CREATING THE PALESTINIAN STATE

CREATING THE PALESTINIAN STATE
A Strategy for Peace

Jerome M. Segal

LAWRENCE HILL BOOKS

Library of Congress Cataloging-in-Publication Data

Segal, Jerome M. , 1943–
  Creating the Palestinian state.

  1. Palestine--Politics and government--1948–
2. Jewish-Arab relations--1973–   . I. Title.
II. Title: Palestinian state.
DS119.7.S38167 1989   956.94'05   88–32802
ISBN 1-55652-050-6
ISBN 1-55652-055-7 (pbk.)

Printed in the United States of America
First edition
First printing
Published by Lawrence Hill Books
An Imprint of Chicago Review Press, Incorporated
814 North Franklin Street
Chicago, Illinois 60610
ISBN 1-55652-055-7

*For my Mother and Father
and Etta and Esther*

Contents

Preface

This is not your typical book on the Israeli-Palestinian conflict. It is not a history of the conflict. It is not an analysis of one of the many aspects of the conflict. It is a strategy proposal for resolving the conflict.

A strategy for resolving the conflict is not the same as a description of the post-conflict political landscape. A strategy proposal prescribes steps for getting to the post-conflict situation. It offers a plan of action for achieving conflict resolution.

In the vast literature on the Middle East, it is amazing how few attempts there have been to lay out in detail any strategy for resolving the conflict. What exists are typically strategy proposals directed towards either the Israelis or the Americans.

This manuscript is a strategy proposal directed primarily towards the Palestinians. In the first instance it is directed towards the Palestine Liberation Organization (PLO). But the PLO, like all political actors, does not operate in a vacuum. It cannot by fiat pick up one strategy and drop another. It operates within a network of constraints and influences. The strategic decisions it makes are affected by the views and likely responses of the other actors: the Palestinian people, the Israeli government, the Israeli people, the American government, the American people, the Arab nations, the Soviet Union, the European states, and so forth. In particular, there is a major role to be played by the American Jewish community.

Thus, while this proposal is in the first instance directed towards the PLO and the Palestinians, it is also crucially directed at the wider community of actors. Essentially, it is a strategy for bringing about peace through the two-state solution. It seeks a peace based on the idea of partition, an idea that forty years ago was supported by Israel, the United States, and the Soviet Union.

Forty years ago, the Arab world rejected the two-state solution. Today the PLO is seeking peace based on the two-state idea. The strategy it has been following calls for the convening of an international conference and for negotiations. To a very large extent, once it became abundantly obvious that Israel could not be defeated militarily, virtually everyone assumed that the only alternative was negotiations. A great deal of heat has been generated over the issue of whether the venue for these negotiations should be an international conference, multilateral efforts along the Camp David model, or direct bilateral talks.

The strategy proposal I put forward does not place the negotiations process at the center of activity. I see negotiations as coming late in the process. I see negotiations as likely to bring a formal peace only when they are negotiations between two states: Israel and Palestine. For this to be possible, there must first exist a Palestinian state. Creating the Palestinian state without obtaining prior Israeli agreement lies at the heart of this strategy.

I believe it can be done. But it cannot be done by the Palestinians alone. It can only occur if there is broad support from all who seek peace along the lines of the two-state solution. It is toward building this consensus that this analysis is directed.

A sketch of my strategy for creating a Palestinian state first appeared on April 27, 1988 in Arabic in *Al-Quds*, the largest Arabic newspaper published in Jerusalem. It met with widespread interest within the territories and was the subject of a few news stories. Versions of that article appeared in English in *Al-Fajr*, *The Washington Post*, the *International Herald Tribune*, and other papers.

This book lays out the strategy in detail. As this manuscript progressed, I sent sections of it to people in the territories and to the PLO leadership in Tunis. The core of the manuscript was available by the end of June 1988.

In early August 1988 public attention to my proposals took a quantum leap forward, propelled by two events. The first was the decision by King Hussein of Jordan to abandon Jordan's claim to the West Bank, thereby formally submerging the "Jordanian option." And the second was the revelation that Israeli authorities had found a plan for a Palestinian declaration of independence in the East Jerusalem offices of Palestinian leader Faisal Husseini, a man some see as the leader of the Palestinian uprising.

When the news of the so-called "Husseini-document" broke in Israel, it was quickly observed that the text and conceptual framework of that document strongly resembled the strategy I had advanced in *Al-Quds*. Thus, overnight I became a sensation within Israel and was referred to as "the Herzl of the Palestinian state" or "the Jewish father of the Palestinian state." There is a certain silliness in these descriptions, and they vastly exaggerate the contribution that I, an American Jewish academic, have made. My role has been essentially to conceptualize and articulate a strategy that was already implicit in the praxis of the Palestinian people.

Furthermore, my efforts have been directed towards the creation of a Palestinian state, not primarily as an end in itself, but as a component part of the two-state solution. The two-state solution is, in my estimation, the only basis for a stable peace in the Middle East, and in the long run, the only basis on which the survival of either state can be assured.

This book provides a strategy for resolving the Israeli-Palestinian conflict. It should be judged on a very simple basis: How does it compare to any other proposal for bringing peace and justice to the Middle East?

The Introduction discusses the historical meaning of the Israeli-Palestinian conflict. Chapter one consists of a brief account of the evolution of the PLO. I argue that over the last twenty years the PLO has totally reversed its most basic position. At the outset it was dedicated to Israel's destruction. Today it seeks a Palestinian state that will live at peace with Israel. In Chapter two I sketch the general terms of the proposed strategy. There are four broad components: 1) a unilateral Palestinian Declaration of Independence and Statehood, coupled with the formation of a provisional government that replaces the PLO; 2) a peace initiative; 3) steps to build the inner sinews of the new state; and 4) a campaign to achieve Israeli troop withdrawal. Chapter three details thirteen specific elements of the strategy. Chapter four deals with a vast array of questions and challenges that may be posed.

I wish to thank the Institute for Philosophy and Public Policy, at the University of Maryland, College Park for assistance and support. Thanks also to the editors of *Al-Quds*, *Al-Fajr*, and *The Washington Post* for publishing my first formulations along these lines. And thanks to The Brookings Institution and the Institute for Policy Studies for arranging discussions that allowed me to sharpen my ideas and better understand the perspectives of others.

I also wish to thank David Ludden, Mark Cohen, Ellen Siegel, Naomi Nim, Norbert Hornstein, David Luban, Claudia Mills, Carroll Linkins, and Gershen Baskin for their various contributions.

Introduction
THE HISTORICAL MEANING OF
THE ISRAELI-PALESTINIAN CONFLICT

A Palestinian friend once asked me why I was so involved in the Israeli-Palestinian conflict. In responding to her, it immediately became clear to me, clearer than it had ever been before, how different the conflict is for her, a West Bank Palestinian, than for me, an American Jew.

By this I am not referring to our perceptions of the basic facts of the conflict or our analyses of the options facing both sides. In our case these were quite similar. And in the end we both agreed that the two-state solution is the only viable solution for either people.

The difference that struck me was the extent to which I was absorbed with abstractions, while for her the conflict is remarkably concrete. For her it involves constant contact with the Israeli military. Every day it involves silent contact with the Israeli settlers whose cars cut in front of her at checkpoints along the road from Ramallah to Jerusalem. For her it means the danger of arrest and imprisonment without charge or trial; it means relatives and friends who have been injured or even killed; it means people who have lost the homes they were raised in and the fields that their grandparents tilled.

For me the conflict raises questions of Jewish identity, the meaning of history, and the meaning of Jewish history, in particular. Understandably, she had very little patience for my abstractions. But it is this most abstract level of the conflict that I find compelling, and in its own way deeply personal.

My relationship to Israel began before I had ever heard of the

Palestinians, and certainly prior to any understanding of the history and nature of the conflict. I grew up in a totally Jewish neighborhood in the Bronx. After I finished regular school hours, I would go for an extra hour of instruction at the local Yiddish school. The instruction was not of a religious nature. We were there to learn Jewish history, to learn to read, speak, and write in Yiddish, to learn Yiddish songs and a smattering of Hebrew. In a word, we were there because our parents wanted to make sure that we developed a strong Jewish identity.

There was a time every year when we went door-to-door in the neighborhood selling stamps and collecting money that would be used to plant trees in Israel. It never occurred to anyone to ask why we were doing this, or what our relationship to Israel was. Israel wasn't a central preoccupation; it was part of the landscape. Raising money for Israel was just an accepted part of childhood.

When the 1967 war occurred, I was no longer a child. For three years I had participated with millions of others in the effort to extricate the United States from Vietnam. I had published and lectured on the nature of moral agency and on selective conscientious objection. Philosophically, I was broadly critical of any form of soldiering. I saw it as a process whereby one participated in the dehumanization of the other, where one made oneself into someone indifferent to or even proud of causing the deaths of other young people little different from oneself.

Yet when the Six Day War occurred, these philosophic conclusions evaporated. I found myself thrilled by Israel's victories. I reacted to the news reports of fighting in the Middle East with full enthusiasm for an Israeli triumph; mine was the kind of total identification with war that I found appalling when I encountered it anywhere else.

Fifteen years later, when Israel invaded Lebanon, I joined with other Jews to protest in front of the Israeli embassy in Washington. I protested not merely because the Lebanon war was an optional war. And it was not merely that I expected the war to be a disaster for Israel. It was something much stronger—a growing sense that Israel had gone deeply astray. It was the realization that the Palestinians also have rights and valid claims, and that as a people they have been and continue to be the primary victims of the Israeli-Palestinian conflict. It was the realization that the conflict continued in large part because something very significant was wrong in the Jewish community and within Israel: we were refusing in principle to extend to others the same rights we claimed for ourselves. It was then, in 1982, that I became active in the Jewish peace movement in the United States.

My engagement in the Israeli-Palestinian conflict turns on an essentially conceptual point: Jewish identity and Jewish history have become hostage to this conflict. Who and what we are will be determined by this conflict and the relationship we bear to it.

We are all creatures within a larger human story; our identity is in large measure determined by the meaning of that story and our role within it. To understand ourselves in relation to the Middle East conflict we must understand its historical meaning.

To ask about the historical meaning of the Israeli-Palestinian conflict is to ask about its larger significance. Larger in the sense of bearing on more than the interests of the immediate participants, the 1.5 million Palestinians living in the West Bank and Gaza, the 100,000 Jewish settlers, the over 3 million Israeli Jews, the 500,000 Arab citizens of Israel, the 400,000 Palestinians living in Lebanon, the PLO members scattered around the Middle East, and the wider circles of Palestinians and Jews around the globe.

When a question of this sort is put, it most often is a question of whether or not the conflict can affect still wider interests. And indeed, there is no doubt that it can and has. To see this one has only to make a list of areas of past and possible future impacts:
  –oil prices
  –nuclear proliferation
  –Arab unity
  –U.S.-Soviet trade/detente
  –U.S.-Soviet conflict
  –U.S. relations with the Islamic world
  –the Iran-Iraq war

–American politics

–South Africa

–Jewish-Black relations in the U.S.

In one sense, these are the crucial arenas that make this conflict so important and make it absolutely necessary for any future U.S. President to set a resolution of the conflict high on the list of foreign policy priorities.

Yet these are not the factors I have in mind when I raise the question of the historical meaning of the Israeli-Palestinian conflict. The question I am asking has less to do with the causal consequences of the conflict, even the causal consequences for humanity, than it has to do with how this conflict affects the very meaning of history.

The question of the historical meaning of the Israeli-Palestinian conflict is a question about how what happens in this conflict will give one or another kind of meaning to human history, how it will force us to reperceive central aspects of the human story, how it will cause us to change our understanding of ourselves as human beings.

Put in this fashion it sounds as if there is only one story of human history. Surely this is not correct. Potentially there are an infinite number of such stories, but not all stories are on the same level. Some stories are more comprehensive than others; they offer a perspective that makes sense of a wide variety of events. Some stories are more powerful than others. Some are so powerful that once one has heard them, one forever defines oneself in relation to them. Indeed, it is by learning such stories of human history that one learns who one is.

The telling of such a story is a projection of one's values, a projection of one's concerns, of what one cares about and is moved by. Our values are reflected in how we choose the subject of the story and in the transformations we judge worthy of attention. Once importance is established, the dramatic character of history returns, for drama is nothing other than an account of what is important that is filled with uncertainty.

The story I am concerned with is clearly a Jewish story. It is also a Christian story, and as such bears some important connection to an account of history that a Muslim might hold. It is very much a Western story and might seem of less significance to the three-quarters of the planet that have evolved largely in isolation from the West. In the end it might be little more than a personal statement, yet I believe it to have universal significance, to be a central text for humanity as a whole.[1]

Who is the "we" that the story is about? Ultimately, that depends on who is listening to the story and how he or she listens. It is a matter of whether or not the listener finds in it something that tells him about himself.

On one level the primary subject of the story starts out as the Jews. Only toward the end do the Palestinians enter. Yet because the Jews are representative of all human suffering, the story of the Jews is allegorically the story of the Palestinians. And in the end the encounter of the Jews and the Palestinians is the encounter of each people with itself at another point in time. For the Jews of Israel, the Palestinians of today and especially the Palestinian victims of tomorrow's expulsion are all the Jewish victims of history. And for the Palestinians, the Jews of Israel are what a suffering people becomes when it becomes a state. They are in potentia Palestinians of a possible future.

Who are the Jews? They are the only people of the ancient world of Western civilization to have survived as a coherent entity from their emergence roughly thirty-five hundred years ago. Of other ancient peoples we have traces, descendants, and in some cases abundant knowledge. But they themselves are all gone. There are nowhere to be found ancient Egyptians, Mycenaens, Sumerians; ancient Greeks, Romans, or Babylonians. For the West, the Jews are the only living thread that has endured from the earliest times of which we have records.

They were the most historical people ever to exist. They imposed upon history a particular story. They were the first really to think of history as a story. They were not the first to have creation myths, but the first to have a vision of what happened to themselves in history and to see this as the story of the world.

The ancient Greeks saw history as cyclical. For the Jews each historical moment was unique, never to be repeated. History was God-endowed. It begins with a specific moment of creation. Human subjects were central to its unfolding, and human actions were the driving force of historical change. History would be the one-time story that begins with the creation of Adam and Eve and their expulsion from paradise and ends with the coming of the Messiah and the millennium.

The Jews are a numerically small people; today less than one-half of one percent of the global population. Yet from them emerged many of the central figures who have shaped human experience; Abraham, Moses, Jesus of Nazareth, Karl Marx, Sigmund Freud, Albert Einstein. They are the most literate people; their rites of passage consist of reading from sacred texts. And the texts themselves are less theologies than they are histories.

Morally and religiously the Jews carried ideas and perceptions that have formed much of modern consciousness. They were monotheistic; they emphasized social justice and concern for the poor.

But more than anything else the Jews became the people of suffering, the victims of the world. And in resistance to this victimization they developed a will to survive as a people that transformed their suffering into a strength that helped them to endure. And they did this through historical interpretation. They recorded the facts of the catastrophes that befell them as a people; they interpreted these facts to find some meaning in them; they wove these histories into religious ceremonies containing memories even of what befell them three thousand years ago. And they built the identity of each generation around an understanding of this extended history.

Early on they lived for hundreds of years in conditions of servitude in ancient Egypt. Somehow they managed to break away, as an entire people. They invaded the land that is today Israel and the West Bank, and with great ruthlessness killed and drove out the inhabitants. And for hundreds of years they went about their business and contended with more powerful neighbors. In 586 B.C., they suffered an enormous defeat at the hands of the Babylonians and yet managed to survive and return and reestablish a state. Through mistakes that probably could have been avoided, they ultimately found themselves in a death struggle with Roman armies, in which they were finally defeated, killed, and dispersed.

Over the next two thousand years they survived as a distinct people. Many lived in Europe under rulers committed to a faith that centered on one of their great teachers, but one whom they disowned. So long as the Roman Empire existed, the dispersed Jews retained rights as citizens of the super-state. But as the empire ceased to exist, they were no longer seen as citizens, but merely as foreigners. Ultimately within the medieval framework they came to be viewed as the property of local rulers. Devoid of rights, they could be expelled at will.

Large numbers continued to live in the Middle East. They came under the control of Moslem rulers, whose religion also saw itself as emerging from the Jewish tradition, but was far less hostile to it than Christianity. Yet here too they were outsiders, guests, soujourners without an equal claim to the earth they inhabited.

Ironically, it was the Crusades, the great conflict over the Middle East, the conflict between the Christian and the Islamic world, that was the cause of intensified Jewish suffering, as crusading hordes destroyed the Jewish communities they found in their path as they moved towards Jerusalem.

Centuries of intense vulnerability ensued, and then with the Enlightenment came the French Revolution and Napolean, the would-be world emperor. And under Napoleon, for the first time in over a thousand years, European Jews became citizens of the lands in which they lived. Ironically, this very acceptance tended to undermine their identity, and in some quarters even religious observances were changed to fit in with Christian traditions.

Jews entered more and more fully into the life of Europe. But the spirit of enlightenment was not to last, and anti-Semitism emerged stronger than ever. Within the Jewish community, there was internal struggle as diverse elements–the orthodox, the Jewish-nationalists, the socialists–contended for the soul of the people. The nationalists began their project of bringing about Jewish sovereignty over a piece of territory, of creating a Jewish state. They sought the ancient territories of the Middle East, then ruled by European colonial powers. They entreated with these powers, paying little heed to the people living there. But those people too were struggling to emerge from the yoke of foreign rule; they too were awakening to a call for national self-determination. So conflict evolved between the immigrant Zionists and the Palestinians. And they slew each other, each anticipating that soon the colonial rulers would leave.

And in Europe, the Europe of Christianity and the Enlightenment, there emerged an evil that surpassed anything ever seen before. The Jews underwent the worst catastrophe of their thirty-five hundred year existence. Yet three years after the Nazi horror had ended, the Jewish-nationalist project had triumphed. The colonial power had withdrawn and for the first time in two thousand years the Jews were sovereign over a territory. But the conflict with the Palestinians continued, and after two decades the newly sovereign Jews became rulers over a large Palestinian population in the West Bank and Gaza. And after twenty years of Israeli occupation, the Palestinians rose up in massive revolt.

And so the conflict continues. Where will it end? What meaning will the ending give to the thirty-five hundred year history? What meaning will it give to the two thousand years of oppression? What meaning will it give to the six million who went into the ovens? And how will the potential alternative endings affect the meaning of the human story that began with Abraham and Moses and then Jesus Christ and later Mohammed?

Consider the meaning of three alternative endings:

Destruction of the Other

The Uprising that began in late 1987 continued. After several hundred Palestinians were killed and after alternating periods of relative calm and new outbursts, it looked as if the Israeli government had succeeded in restoring its authority. Then, just as it appeared that order had been restored, an Israeli soldier was fatally knifed. He died. Another was killed a day later. In Jerusalem a young girl was killed. Settlers in the territories took matters into their own hands: three Arab villages were attacked, thirty houses were burned, and seven people were killed. A week later, in reprisal there was the first attack on a Jewish settlement in the West Bank, killing eight Israelis and six Palestinians; settlers reacted with another attack on nearby villages. Individual young people who had previously thrown stones began escalating the level of violence. Over the next several months, the level of violence continued to rise. The Israeli army ordered an entire village evacuated and moved in with tractors to demolish it. Soldiers were attacked by young Palestinians who remained in the village. Fighting ensued for several days before all the villagers either fled or were killed.

Israel was condemned around the world. Cries of "Warsaw Ghetto in reverse" were heard. Attacks on soldiers and settlers erupted throughout the territories. Inside Israel the political pressure to take action became enormous. The stage for the Expulsion was set. Without warning Israeli troops entered Jordan and secured a ten square mile area. Inside the territories, the army moved with speed and full force. Airplanes were used to strafe villages and West Bank cities. After twenty-four hours the entire population was in a state of panic. On foot, by car, and by Israeli bus and truck West Bank villagers were expelled from one town after another. In each area some Palestinians resisted. They were simply isolated, as the army pressed the expulsion forward. Within three weeks, the West Bank had been depopulated. The army then systematically began a mopping up operation. In village after village tanks were used against defenders. They fought hard and most died fighting. The death toll came to twenty thousand Palestinians and eight hundred Israeli soldiers.

While the Arab world screamed and Israel was condemned, no one intervened. Egypt broke off diplomatic relations but did not go to war. Inside Israel Meir Kahane was celebrated as the prophet of the final solution. But the solution proved unstable.

After two years King Hussein of Jordan was assassinated, and his regime fell to a Palestinian revolution. Following the Israeli expulsion Jordan was overwhelmingly Palestinian, and the expulsion had totally radicalized the population. The Iran-Iraq war had come to an end. In the aftermath of the Palestinian revolution in Jordan, an Iraq-Jordan political union was formed. Israel now faced a hostile and powerful Iraqi-Jordanian alliance equipped with chemical weapons, a hostile Syria with topflight Soviet weapons, and a hostile Egypt. War was inevitable. The Israelis struck first and did tremendous damage, but unlike previous wars, this one continued on and on. Gradually the Arab forces regained their strength and started to use their great numbers. Egypt had a population of fifty million, Iraq-Jordan of twenty million, Syria of ten million. Dangerously pressed Israel had no choice but to resort to nuclear weapons, first used on Baghdad, then on Damascus and Cairo. Ultimately it broke the back of Arab resistance. The immediate effect of the nuclear attacks killed nine million people, six million in Cairo alone. The effect of radiation killed another five million. Israeli casualties were high, but in the end Israel emerged victorious. The dead were everywhere. The Palestinians were gone forever.

Mutual Destruction

During the course of the war, Pakistan secretly delivered nuclear weapons to Libya, fulfilling a pledge made years before when Libya helped fund the development of "the Islamic bomb." After the Israeli nuclear strike, Libya launched a nuclear attack on Israel. One missile hit Tel Aviv; another hit Haifa. A cloud of radiation settled over Jerusalem. Over two million Israelis died; the Israeli Defense Forces were not destroyed in full. They retaliated against Libya. While Cairo had been hit, most of the Egyptian forces were still intact. Six months later they crossed the Sinai and overran Israel. The United States stayed on the sidelines. The Jewish state had been destroyed. Radiation had made the area virtually uninhabitable for both Palestinian and Jew.

Mutual Recognition of the Other

After the Israeli elections of 1988, Israel surprised the world by announcing that it was prepared to hold open elections in the West Bank and Gaza to determine who represented the Palestinians. The Israelis committed themselves to negotiate with any leadership elected by the population so long as it renounced the use of terrorism and recognized Israel's right to exist. In the elections, the Palestinians almost unanimously voted for a PLO slate. The Israeli government balked and specified that the PLO would have to renounce terrorism and recognize Israel's right to exist, but that if it did, then Israel would negotiate with the elected figures. The PLO issued a statement saying that it opposed all forms of terrorism including state terrorism, and that it was prepared to negotiate a permanent peace with Israel. The Israeli government announced that it regarded the PLO statement as sufficient.

Israel opened negotiations with PLO representatives in the context of an international conference. The negotiations were difficult and seemingly interminable, but ultimately Israel agreed to a gradual process whereby the Palestinians eventually would have their own state in the West Bank and Gaza. The Palestinians in turn agreed to a wide array of provisions designed to insure Israeli security once the new state was established.

The PLO, signing for the Palestinians, announced that the conflict had been resolved in all its dimensions. There were dissenting voices but they were isolated. Jordan and Syria similarly negotiated with Israel under the international conference umbrella. A peace treaty with Jordan was achieved, and Syria settled for a demilitarization of the Golan Heights. The agreements took hold. A major development effort for the region was undertaken. The economies of Jordan, Palestine, and Israel became more and more interdependent and some form of economic union was achieved. Over time reconciliation of a sort was accomplished. Peace was secured.

These scenarios are examples of what I take to be the only possible endings. Either 1) the Israelis will destroy all of their enemies and eliminate the Palestinians, or 2) the Israelis and their enemies ultimately will destroy each other, or 3) the conflict will be resolved along the lines of the two-state solution.

The first two endings to the story are monstrous, but they are all too possible. In the first scenario a Jewish state emerges for the first time in about two thousand years, and then within fifty years, the new state, the expression of a brilliant and long-suffering people, a teacher to the nations, degenerates first into an occupying army, and then into an oppressor nation. Unrestrained by any compassion for the other, unrestrained by memories of its own suffering, it crushes the weak, and girds for future conflicts.

The decimation of the Palestinians leads the Israelis deeper into hell. They incinerate the Arab world and emerge the perpetrators of a new Holocaust. After thirty-five hundred years of suffering nothing has been learned. Jewish moral stature is revealed as a weak reed that depended for its existence on powerlessness. The centuries produced no lasting transformation; as a state Israel was like any other state; the foreigner did not count. In the end the great tale produced nothing. The slave is really the master waiting his turn. Such is history.

The second story ends with joint incineration. Within fifty years of the liberation of Auschwitz, millions of Jews again perish in the flames. This time they take millions with them to their deaths. This time they bear a good part of the responsibility themselves. In the end, the Jewish will to survive is itself destroyed. Such is history and the sad story of the Jewish encounter with the world, and the world's encounter with this remarkable people.

And then there is the third relatively happy ending, where somehow sanity triumphs, and a way is found for mutual accommodation. In the end, the Jewish leaders see the stark alternatives of either becoming mass murderers or succumbing to mass murder. Drawing on a moral strength and a will to survive they reject both alternatives, risking a Palestinian state and relinquishing land they have come to view as their own. It is their decisive historical choice, and they make the right one.

In exact detail none of these scenarios will occur, but over time something similar to one of them will come to pass. Hopefully, it will be some variant of the last ending. It is to this purpose that this book is directed.

I do not believe that the two-state solution will emerge in the way I have described above. In the above tale, the Israelis come to their senses before it is too late. I do not think that this will happen. The Jewish encounter with the world has left Israelis too shattered to make sound policy. If a cataclysm in the Middle East is to be avoided, some other actor must be found.

I believe that this actor is the Palestinian people themselves. I believe that it is possible for them to become the master of what is now a mindless process heading toward destruction.

As the central actors in the final stages of the historical drama, the Palestinians can accomplish something for themselves, for the world, and ultimately and ironically for the Jewish people, that will not otherwise be achieved. They can unilaterally impose the two-state solution and bring peace to the Middle East.

This book is essentially a plan of action. It is not a value-free analysis of the Middle East. No doubt, it contains errors. I hope they are small ones. Essentially it is directed to the Palestinians and toward the central role in world history which is theirs to play, if they will.

Some have called it arrogant for a Jew to write a strategy for the Palestinians. No doubt it is that. But there is another way of looking at it as well. It can be seen as a plea for help. The struggle for an independent Palestinian state is also the struggle for a humane and safe Israel. As there can be no Judaism without a commitment to justice, it is also a struggle for Jewish history and the Jewish future. It is a struggle in which Jews and Palestinians must find each other as allies.

Notes: Introduction

[1]In this it is like asking of the Holocaust, "Who did it happen to?" Most immediately it happened to the Jews of Europe, but it can also be viewed as something that happened to all of Europe, to all of Western civilization, or ultimately, something that happened to humanity, something that throws a penetrating light on the nature of human beings and on what has happened to us on this planet.

Chapter 1
THE EVOLUTION OF THE PLO

Common wisdom in the United States is that the Israeli-Palestinian conflict continues because of the fundamental unwillingness of the Palestine Liberation Organization (PLO) to make peace with Israel. A typical lament is that "there is no one to negotiate with." If Palestinian "moderates" are mentioned, the response is that whenever there has been a "moderate" Palestinian willing to make peace with Israel, he has been assassinated.

The story is not accurate. To see this, one only has to ask a simple question: "What do you mean by moderate?" For most people, a moderate Palestinian is one who is prepared to live at peace with Israel if he or she can do so in a state of his own. A further mark of a moderate is that he wants the PLO to enter into negotiations with the Israelis to achieve a peace based on the two-state solution. But if this is the definition of moderate, then Arafat is a moderate, and, as we shall see, so is the Palestine National Council (the highest decision making body of the PLO). That the myth of PLO intransigence is believed so strongly reflects not only an effective public relations effort by the Israeli government, but an astonishing failure on the part of the PLO to communicate the gradual but significant transformation in its outlook over the years.

Of course, this is more than a communications failure; there are conflicting messages, deep ambivalences, and a strong tendency to emphasize the continuity of present and past policies rather than to call attention to major policy shifts. This style of denial, which tends to obscure rather than to take full advantage of change, has deep and complex roots. I do not pretend to understand it fully, but at least one dimension of the explanation

15

has to do with honor, pride, and dignity. Once one accepts the fact that the Palestinians have essentially lost a fight to hold onto lands that they quite naturally believed were their own, and that they have lost quite badly, the tactics and style of the PLO become less mysterious.

When the outside observer identifies aspects of the Palestinian struggle as counterproductive, it is worth remembering that implicit in this notion is a definition of the objective of the struggle. One significant component of what the Palestinian resistance has been about, even if the Palestinians do not frequently articulate this to themselves, is that it is a search for a way to bear defeat with dignity. This is not to say that this is all the struggle is about. It is clearly an effort to prevent further defeat, to prevent dispossession from the West Bank and Gaza. It is a struggle to recover from some aspects of prior defeats; in particular for Palestinians to emerge from a stateless refugee status to citizens of a Palestinian state. And on the aspirational level it reflects a desire to reverse past defeats and to return to lost lands.

For the Palestinians, gaining their own state and ending their refugee status remains something to be attained in the future. But participation in the Palestinian resistance, be it from within the PLO or simply on the streets of West Bank villages, provides Palestinians with something of great importance in the present. To resist, to fight back, to deny defeat–these are not merely organizational positions but human stances that provide the individual with self-respect, even in the face of disaster. Strategies and tactics that are perceived as involving a further loss of dignity are rejected because they undermine the little that there is to preserve.

While the issues of dignity, honor, and pride imbue the Palestinian struggle against Israel with rich symbolic content, there is also a pragmatic side to the struggle which corresponds to the hope that some measure of recovery from past defeat is possible and to the fear that future disasters may dwarf those of the past. It is this pragmatic component that has motivated the transformation of the PLO over the years.

The magnitude of this transformation should be obvious

from the simple fact that in recent years disputes within the PLO have erupted over such questions as whether it should participate in negotiations as part of a joint Jordanian-Palestinian delegation or insist on being represented as a completely separate entity. Yet even the Palestinian willingness to negotiate has not been fully perceived by most Israelis or Americans.

It is useful to review some of the key points in the transformation that the PLO has undergone since the 1960s.

The PLO Rejection of Resolution 242

In 1967, following the Six-Day War, the United Nations Security Council adopted Resolution 242. This Resolution, supported by both the United States and the Soviet Union, emphasized "the inadmissibility of the acquisition of territory by war" and then went on to identify two principles on which peace in the Middle East should be based:

1. Withdrawal of Israeli armed forces from territories occupied in the recent conflict;

2. Termination of all claims or states of belligerency and respect for and acknowledgement of the sovereignty, territorial integrity and political independence of every State in the area and their right to live in peace within secure and recognized boundaries free from threats or acts of force.[1]

The day after the resolution was passed the PLO issued a statement rejecting it and itemizing the reasons for rejection. Among these, it identified as "the most important. . .that the Security Council ignores the existence of the Palestinian people and their right to self-determination."[2]

But there was also another reason offered in that 1967 statement:

The resolution more than once refers to Israel's right to exist and to establish permanent, recognized frontiers. It also refers to Israel's safety and security and to her being freed from threats, and in general to the termination of the state of belligerency with her. All this imposes on the Arab countries undertakings and a political and actual situation which are fundamentally and gravely inconsistent with the Arab character of Palestine, the essence of the Palestine cause and the right of the Palestinians to their homeland.[3]

Given the changes that have occurred since, and the fact that today Yasser Arafat says that the PLO accepts Resolution 242 with certain provisos, it is important to remember that the original rejection of this resolution was tied to a fundamental rejection of Israel.

The PLO Covenant, 1968

In the year following the adoption of Resolution 242, the PLO Covenant took on its now famous form. The Covenant was explicit in its rejection of Israel. Article 1 stipulated that "Palestine is the homeland of the Palestinian Arab people,"[4] and Article 2 specified that "Palestine with its boundaries that existed at the time of the British mandate is an integral regional unit. . . ."[5] Article 15 spoke of the duty to "repulse the Zionist, Imperialist invasion from the great Arab homeland and to purge the Zionist presence from Palestine."[6] And Article 19 stated that "The partitioning of Palestine in 1947 and the establishment of Israel is fundamentally null and void, whatever time has elapsed."[7]

Thus, within the framework of the Covenant there is nothing to negotiate with Israel except its destruction. The Covenant rules out any possibility of reaching a peace settlement with Israel. Moreover, since the very idea of negotiating with Israel appears to imply recognition of its existence and a willingness to come to terms with it, Article 9 states that, "Armed struggle is the only way to liberate Palestine and is therefore a strategy and not tactics."[8] And Article 21 states, "The Palestinian Arab people, in expressing itself through the armed revolution, rejects every solution that is a substitute for a complete liberation of Palestine, and rejects all plans that aim at the settlement of the Palestine issue or its internationalization."[9]

The PLO has not revised the Covenant since these passages were adopted in 1968. Instead it has simply chosen to ignore them. As a deliberate organizational style, one which is not without serious damage to the Palestinian cause, the PLO tends to minimize the extent to which it has changed. Tactically nothing could have served Israeli hardliners better than for the PLO to have tried to disguise the extent of its transformation.

For a quick overview, the evolution of the PLO can be viewed in relation to the major wars. Three periods can be marked out:

–From the 1967 defeat to the 1973 war.

–From 1973 to the Lebanon war in 1982.

–From 1982 to the present.

From 1967 to 1973: Militancy

The Arab defeat in 1967 discredited the Arab regimes and the prior leadership of the PLO. It was at this time that the PLO became essentially a Palestinian organization under the leadership of Yasser Arafat. From 1967 to 1973 the PLO sought to establish itself as the sole representative of the Palestinian people and to block any efforts to reach an accord with Israel in exchange for a Palestinian state on the West Bank and Gaza.

During this period one of the most noteworthy occurrences, pregnant with implications for the future, was a shift in the PLO's approach to the Jewish population of Israel. Article 6 of the Covenant states that "Jews who were living permanently in Palestine until the beginning of the Zionist invasion will be considered Palestinians."[10] The "beginning of the Zionist invasion" has been understood as meaning the year 1917. The implication of this was that other Jews living in Israel were there illegitimately and would have to leave, if and when a Palestinian victory over Israel was achieved. A critique of this position emerged from the left wing elements of the PLO, from groups most militantly opposed to any negotiations with Israel. Thus, one document submitted by the Democratic Front for the Liberation of Palestine (DFLP) to the sixth PNC in 1969 proposed:

2. the rejection of chauvinistic solutions of Palestinian or Arab origin (massacring the Jews, driving them into the sea, and so on);

3. a popular democratic solution to the Palestine and Israeli problem. . . . Such a solution would mean the setting up of a popular democratic Palestinian state for Arabs and Jews alike in which there would be no discrimination and no room for class or national subjugation and in which the right of both Arabs and

Jews to perpetuate and develop their indigenous cultures would be respected. . . .

5. national liberation, which would be the result of a long popular armed struggle and the total liberation of Palestine, would involve:

the establishment of a democratic state in which Arabs and Jews shall enjoy equal national rights and responsibilities.[11]

The recognition that the Jews have national rights in Palestine provides the logical basis for the further claim that, like all nations, they have a right to self-determination in Palestine and thus a right to a state of their own in Palestine.[12] These, of course, were conclusions that the DFLP did not draw, but a willingness to allow all Jews to remain in a "liberated Palestine" and to have equal rights with Arabs carries powerful implications.

At the same time, within Fatah, (the largest component organization belonging to the PLO), there were those that argued that all Jews should be accepted in a liberated Palestine. Arafat at one point in 1969 spoke of "the 1,259,000 Arabs of the Jewish faith who live in what is now the State of Israel."[13] Here he was referring to the small number of Jews who have always resided in Palestine, plus the very large wave of recent immigrants to Israel from Middle Eastern countries.

This position on the continued Jewish presence within a liberated Palestine was adopted by the eighth PNC in 1971, which asserted:

The armed struggle of the Palestinian people is not a racial or religious struggle directed against the Jews. That is why the future state that will be set up in Palestine liberated from Zionist imperialism will be a democratic Palestinian state. All who wish to will be able to live in peace there with the same rights and the same duties. . . .[14]

This change became a permanent part of the PLO framework. In current PLO publications containing the text of the Covenant there is only one asterisk. It appears next to Article 6 and it reads:

Since the adoption of the Palestine National Charter, policy on this point has been changed and is best expressed by the 1974 statement to the UN General Assembly by the Chairman of the PLO Executive Committee, Yasser Arafat, which has been endorsed by the Palestine National Council. The relevant extract reads: When we speak of our common hopes for the Palestine of tomorrow, we include in our perspective all Jews now living in Palestine who choose to live with us there in peace and without discrimination . . . that we might live together in a framework of a just peace in our democratic Palestine. [15]

As mentioned before, the period prior to the 1973 war, following the complete rout of the Arab armies in 1967, was the period of the greatest PLO militancy. It may seem illogical that Palestinian militancy should be at its height following the most convincing demonstration of Israeli power, and that greater moderation should follow the 1973 war that drove the Israelis back from the Suez Canal. But the Palestinian resistance has never followed a logic predicated on the calm assessment of costs, benefits, probabilities, and risks. Rather, it has followed the deeper logic of a resistance movement that has been above all else a way of retaining Palestinian dignity in Palestinian eyes.

Following the 1967 disaster, the PLO staked out the most unlikely fantasies of future power. Anyone who argued for more moderate objectives on pragmatic grounds was seen as a threat.

The character of this period emerges in the following statement by Arafat in 1970:

> The American-Israeli scheme is at present trying to establish a Palestinian state linked with Israel.
>
> This is the insidious theme they are harping on: you have had enough fighting, enough battles. The only solution of the Palestinian problem is to establish a Palestinian state in the West Bank or the West Bank and Gaza Strip.
>
> This is the most dangerous proposal that could be made. In the name of the Palestinian revolution, I hereby declare that we shall oppose the establishment of this state to the last member of the Palestinian people, for if ever such a state is established it will spell the end of the whole Palestinian cause.[16]

The eighth PNC, held in 1971, confirmed the Palestinian rejection of a Palestinian state in the West Bank and Gaza. In explaining this rejection, Abu Iyad, a top leader of Fatah, explained, "to accept the state would mean accepting the defeat of the 20 previous years and hence the existence of Israel."[17] Abu Iyad was not inaccurate in his assessment of the meaning of accepting a West Bank/Gaza state. And whenever the details of Middle East diplomacy become confusing it is useful to remember that basic point. The PLO was born a rejectionist organization; to make peace with Israel, even in exchange for a Palestinian state is to have failed in its original objective.

Of course, accepting a state on the West Bank and Gaza as the result of a process of negotiations with Israel was viewed as totally different from militarily gaining control of the West Bank without making peace with Israel. And with a recklessness that is only possible when leaders do not have the responsibility of protecting a territory and population, the maximum imaginable fantasy of power was put forward, in this case by the Democratic Front for the Liberation of Palestine (DFLP):

> In the event that the nightmare of the occupation is ended on the West Bank, our people will not allow its reconquest by the terrorist government of national treason; it will form (on the West Bank) a liberated zone which will serve as a base of revolutionary support to the struggle for the downfall of the traitor regime, and the building of a national regime in the whole of Jordan, and will be a necessary step in the pursuit of the armed struggle to liberate the whole of the national territory and put an end to the Israeli entity.[18]

This scenario contemplated not only wresting control of the West Bank and the Gaza Strip from Israel, but also bringing down Hussein's regime and taking over Jordan. The gap between aspirations and the resources available for their fulfillment could not have been greater.

The strong reaction against the idea of a West Bank state which would be part of a settlement with Israel reflected the fact that even in 1967 this idea was being taken seriously in Palestinian circles. Indeed, immediately after the 1967 war, fifty West Bank leaders actually approached the Israelis with this idea, but they did not find a receptive audience. And in the spring of 1973, months before the October war, President Bourguiba of Tunisia put forward the idea of returning to the 1947 partition plan. This idea was affirmed by the Egyptian government.

Sadat's audacity in launching the 1973 war, and the success of an Arab army in both surprising and driving back the Israelis, had a powerful psychological impact throughout the Arab world. For the Palestinian leadership, it seems to have facilitated a shift from the grandiose objectives that emerged from the total defeat of 1967 to a realization that some sort of minimally adequate settlement might be possible and acceptable. Thus, it appears that in the midst of the 1973 war, Yasser Arafat sent a secret message to Henry Kissinger expressing the PLO's willingness to participate in peace negotiations. In his memoirs, Kissinger writes of a message he received from Arafat on October 10, 1973. He says it,

> ...suggested that the Arabs, having crossed the prewar lines by their own efforts, had regained enough "face" to undertake real negotiations, even if they eventually would lose the battle, as Arafat seemed to predict. According to Arafat, the PLO was willing to participate in these talks though it reserved the right to settle its old score with Jordan.[19]

Assuming that Kissinger's memoirs are accurate, this would be the first point at which the PLO crossed the line and rejected that part of the Covenant which declared that armed struggle was the only way to liberate Palestine. And, of course, to open negotiations with Israel implies a willingness to conclude negotiations–a willingness in other words to make peace with Israel, in total contradiction of the Covenant.

From 1973 to 1982: Internal Struggle

The 1973 war was undertaken by Sadat as a first step towards peace negotiations. He never believed that he could defeat Israel militarily. After the war, peace negotiations were on the international agenda. Faced with the likelihood of negotiations, the PLO was forced to define a realistic stance towards those negotiations. Would they participate or would they be left out? On what terms would they enter? What would they be prepared to accept? A clear PLO position in favor of negotiations did not emerge until many years later. But after the 1973 war the internal debate within the PLO on this issue expanded enormously. It resulted in very different positions being taken by various individuals and factions, and with deep distrust of Arafat on the part of the factions that came to be known as the rejectionists.

One extreme was occupied by PLO figures from Fatah who were personally close to Arafat, in particular, Said Hammami and Dr. Issam Sartawi.

Hammami was the PLO representative in London. In November 1973, just after the war, he published the first of several articles in *The Times*, in which he asserted the right of the Palestinians to participate in any forthcoming peace conference. He continued to speak of a single "binational secular state," but he characterized that goal as an "ultimate solution" that can be created,

> only if and when the two parties genuinely want it and are ready to work for it. . .the first step toward that should be mutual recognition for the two respective parties. The Israeli Jews and the Palestinian Arabs should recognize one another as peoples, with all the rights to which a people is entitled.[20]

Hammami had no organizational mandate to put these ideas forward. Yet he was a PLO representative and remained so for another five years until he was assassinated by the Abu Nidal group. His articles are best seen as a low-risk way for Arafat to test both the internal PLO reaction to such proposals and the Israeli response. Hammami's proposals failed to produce a comparable Israeli response.

At exactly the same time, with the possibility of a Geneva peace conference emerging, several PLO component groups coalesced into the Rejection Front. They affirmed their continued opposition to a Palestinian state, to negotiation, to participation in the Geneva conference, and to any form of settlement that might imply acceptance of Israel.

Stating his opposition to an independent Palestinian state on the West Bank and Gaza, George Habash, leader of the Popular Front for the Liberation of Palestine (PFLP), stated precisely what many today view as the case for such a state:

> Have we realized that this state will be squeezed between Israel on the one side and the reactionary Jordanian regime on the other? Have we realized that this state would be the result of an Arab and international gift? This solution will be the 'final solution' to the Middle East problem.[21]

In short Habash and the rejectionists were merely holding to the basic PLO position articulated in 1968. That they were compelled to form themselves into a Rejection Front demonstrates that there had been a change in mainstream attitudes, however slow and contradictory. And it should be remembered that during this period, prior to the Camp David talks, the Soviets were urging the PLO to participate in a Geneva conference.

As the debate within the PLO continued, one of the verbal formulas that emerged was the idea of "phases"–that an independent national authority on the West Bank made sense so long as it was achieved without any concessions to Israel and was understood as a phase in the struggle for the "liberation of the whole of Palestine." Thus, the twelfth PNC which met in June 1974 adopted a resolution that read:

> The PLO will struggle against any plan for the establishment of a Palestinian entity the price of which is recognition, conciliation, secure borders, renunciation of the national right, and our people's deprivation of their right to return and their right to determine their fate on their national soil.[22]

Clearly, then, Hammami's call for mutual recognition was a

minority position. And it would seem that it had been totally rejected.

Yet another resolution also accepted at the twelfth PNC stated:

> The PLO will struggle by all means, foremost of which is armed struggle, to liberate Palestinian land and to establish the people's national, independent and fighting authority on every part of Palestinian land to be liberated. . . .[23]

If we read this closely we find first that armed struggle has been demoted from its lofty position in the Covenant as "the only means" to the "foremost means," and then we find for the first time a PNC endorsement of the establishment of a Palestinian entity on a part of Palestinian soil. Thus, Habash's warning that the establishment of a Palestinian state would be the end of the effort to "liberate" all of Palestine was rejected.

Did the PNC disagree with Habash's analysis that the geopolitical realities of a mini-state would mean that it was a final solution, not a phase? Or was there a growing tendency to seek a settlement with Israel? Clearly, it was the latter, for Habash's arguments that a mini-state would have to live at peace with Israel are sound and have never been convincingly rebutted. Unfortunately, regardless of its implausibility, the notion that a Palestinian state would be a springboard to further aggression against Israel was seized on by the Israeli opponents of a Palestinian state and became a permanent part of the Israeli brief against dealing with the PLO.

Habash knew that he was losing ground within the center of the PLO, and in September 1974, the PFLP withdrew from the Executive Committee of the PLO. The PFLP statement announcing this decision provides considerable insight into what was happening and, if nothing else, amounted to a demand that the PLO leadership at least be completely open and aboveboard about change. In part it reads:

> 1. After the October war an international and Arab situation came into existence which was favorable to a so-called political settlement of the Arab Israeli conflict. . . . It was perfectly clear what results this settlement was likely to lead to. . . . The price Israel would be paid for withdrawing from all Arab territory would

be . . . steps toward the consolidation of the legality of her existence in the area. . . .

. . .the Palestinian revolution should have submitted to all the Palestinian and Arab masses a precise analysis of this picture and its consequences. . . .

The Palestinian revolution should have revealed the truth about the Geneva conference and the consequences it would lead to. It should have placed itself unambiguously outside the framework of this liquidationist settlement. . . .

The Front has made every effort to ensure (the) rejection of the Geneva conference. . . . But the leadership of the Organization (Arafat) has persistently evaded defining any attitude on the pretext that they have not been officially invited to attend the Geneva conference. . . .

2. . . .At the end of the twelfth session of the Palestine National Council it was clear what the surrenderist leaderships intended –They regarded it as legalizing their pursuit of the course of deviation and surrender. They started to interpret it as they wished, later making statements as they wished, in a manner incompatible with the Organization's charter. . . .

The deception was disclosed and it became clear that what the surrenderist forces were talking of was the tactics misleading fellow-travellers and the masses, rather than misleading the enemy.

3. The leadership of the Liberation Organization started to represent the possibility of its attending the Geneva conference. . . . At a session of the Executive Committee. . .the Executive Committee decided to coordinate with the subservient regime of Jordan.

7. The leadership of the Liberation Organization has denied that any secret contacts have been made with America, the enemy of peoples. But we have established that such secret contacts have been made, without the knowledge of the masses. . . .

Our withdrawal from the Executive Committee is now unavoidable.[24]

Within the first part of this time period, that is, between the 1973 war and the Camp David talks, there occurred the first of a number of meetings between Israelis and PLO members. Initially, they were not officially sanctioned by the PLO. They were known to Arafat, but he had no authorization from the PNC or the Executive Committee to sanction them. In later years, the PNC was to affirm the value of such meetings.

A series of meetings spanned the period from July 1976 to May 1977. The Israeli representation, while not speaking for the government, did contain figures of some prestige, including former General Matti Peled, Arie Eliav, the former secretary-general of the Labour Party and a member of the Knesset, Meir Pail, a member of the Knesset, and Uri Avnery, a respected Israeli journalist. Palestinian representatives included Issam Sartawi, who was close to Arafat, and Sabri Jiryis, a Palestinian intellectual.

In his book, *My Friend, the Enemy,* Uri Avnery relates that at the beginning of 1977 Sartawi consented to the release of a public statement revealing the existence of these talks. It stated, "The PLO is dedicated to the policy of striving for a peaceful solution of the Israel-Palestinian conflict on the basis of mutual acceptance of the principle of freedom, sovereignty and security for both peoples."[25] The statement was not signed by Sartawi and he was not mentioned by name. Still, it created a sensation in Israel. But within days any chance of a breakthrough was destroyed when PLO political offices around the world announced (what was true) that the PLO had not signed any such document, and further asserted that the PLO would never make peace with "the Zionist entity." Avnery says that the Israelis were made to look like liars or dupes. It was clear that the resistance to Sartawi inside the PLO had effectively counterattacked.

Nonetheless, this period just prior to Sadat's visit to Jerusalem must have appeared a promising one to PLO moderates. In March 1977, the thirteenth PNC stressed the right of Palestinians to be represented at Geneva (though recognition of Israel was ruled out), and on March 15, 1977, President Jimmy Carter spoke of the Palestinian right to "a homeland."

While this slow evolution was occurring within the PLO, another development took place which was to control the United States and Israeli government response to such changes and possibilities. In September 1975, a memorandum of agreement was signed by Secretary of State Kissinger and Yigal Allon, the Deputy Prime Minister of Israel, with the prospect of a

Geneva peace conference. The first point stated that, "The Geneva Peace Conference will be reconvened at a time coordinated between the United States and Israel." The second point went on to address U.S. policy toward the PLO:

> The United States will continue to adhere to its present policy with respect to the Palestine Liberation Organization, whereby it will not recognize or negotiate with the Palestine Liberation Organization so long as the Palestine Liberation Organization does not recognize Israel's right to exist and does not accept Security Council Resolutions 242 and 338.[26]

Read within the context of the times, the fact that the Israelis sought this commitment from the United States suggests several things:

1. An awareness of the currents of change within the PLO.

2. A concern that the United States might respond to these by recognizing the PLO.

3. A desire to block this possibility by committing the United States to preconditions for negotiations with the PLO, preconditions that were unlikely to be met by the PLO in advance of negotiations.

Thus, rather than responding favorably to change within the PLO and trying to further this evolution by drawing the PLO to the negotiating table, the Israelis adopted a policy of trying to prevent the PLO from gaining a seat at the table. And in an act of colossal stupidity, Kissinger agreed to handcuff American foreign policy to a rigid stance of refusing to negotiate with the PLO.

On October 1, 1977, the United States and the Soviet Union issued a joint statement identifying component elements of a comprehensive settlement, which included "ensuring the legitimate rights of the Palestinian people." The two governments stated their willingness to participate in international guarantees of the borders between Israel and the neighboring states.

The statement went on to say that:

> The United States and the Soviet Union believe that the only right and effective way for achieving a fundamental solution to all aspects of the Middle East problem in its entirety is negotiations within the framework of the Geneva Peace Conference,

especially convened for these purposes, with participation in its
work of the representatives of all the parties involved in the conflict including those of the Palestinian people. . . .[27]

It concluded by announcing that the United States and the Soviet
Union had decided to reconvene the conference not later than
December 1977.

Given this affirmation and the changes occurring within the
PLO, it is quite likely that the PLO would have found some way
of participating in a reconvened conference. And thus negotiations between the Israelis and the PLO would have finally
begun.

We will never know. Six weeks after the joint U.S.-Soviet
statement, Egyptian President Anwar Sadat stunned the world
by announcing that he was willing to visit Jerusalem. The visit
took place within two weeks. This unilateral willingness to
negotiate directly with the Israelis opened the door to the Camp
David talks, and the intended international conference, which
had gained much momentum, was never held.

Sadat's visit to Jerusalem resulted in a major upsurge of discord within the PLO. The rejectionists claimed that Arafat's
willingness to consider a Geneva conference had paved the way
for Sadat's visit; it was even charged that Arafat had agreed in
advance to Sadat's initiative. In March 1978, still several months
prior to Camp David, the Israelis invaded southern Lebanon.
And during that year, key PLO moderates, including Hammami, were assassinated by the Abu Nidal group, operating out
of Iraq.

The Camp David Accords were signed in the fall of 1978.
They provided for a separate peace treaty with Egypt, with no
provision for a Palestinian state. Throughout the Arab world,
Sadat's perfidy was confirmed. Within the territories
widespread demonstrations of protest erupted against the accords.

In the following four years leading up to Israel's 1982 invasion
of Lebanon, two events should be mentioned as part of this
sketch of PLO evolution toward a concerted effort to undertake
negotiations with Israel. The first is the 1981 ceasefire between
Israel and the PLO negotiated by the United States. The second

is the peace plan put forward by Crown Prince Fahd of Saudi Arabia in August 1981.

In the spring of 1981, Syrian forces in Lebanon attacked Christian Maronite positions, which they feared were part of an effort to link up with Israeli-sponsored Lebanese forces in the south. Israel communicated its unwillingness to allow these attacks by shooting down several Syrian helicopters. In response the Syrians deployed anti-aircraft missiles in the Bakaa valley. The Israelis communicated their intent to take out these missiles. Alarmed at the possibility of a major Israeli-Syrian conflict, the Reagan Administration sent Philip Habib, a retired diplomat, to the area to see if tension could be reduced. Habib met with initial success, as the Israeli and Syrian governments both agreed not to be the first to escalate.

Arguing that it was outside the scope of their talks with Habib, the Israelis carried out a series of attacks on PLO positions in southern Lebanon, and the PLO responded with stepped-up shelling of Israeli towns just over the border. On July 17 and 18, Israeli planes launched a major attack against Palestinian positions in Beirut, with many civilian casualties.

Habib shifted his focus to calming relations between Israel and the PLO. Through a series of indirect negotiations (as the United States would not talk directly with the PLO and both sides wanted to avoid direct Israeli-PLO contact) Habib was able to work out a ceasefire agreement. Though indirect, this agreement represented the first actual negotiated arrangement between Israel and the PLO. By and large it held up until the full-scale Israeli invasion of Lebanon in June 1982.[28]

A few weeks after the ceasefire was arranged, Crown Prince Fahd of Saudi Arabia came forward with a peace plan with these tenets:

1. Israeli evacuation of all Arab territories seized during the 1967 Middle East war, including the Arab sector of Jerusalem.

2. Dismantling the settlements set up by Israel on the occupied lands after the 1967 war.

3. Guaranteeing freedom of religious practices for all religions in the Jerusalem holy shrines.

4. Asserting the rights of the Palestinian people and compensating those Palestinians who do not wish to return to their homeland.

5. Commencing a transitional period in the West Bank of Jordan and the Gaza Strip under United Nations supervision for a duration not exceeding a few months.

6. Setting up a Palestinian State with East Jerusalem as its capital.

7. Affirming the right of all countries of the region to live in peace.

8. Guaranteeing the implementation of these principles by the United Nations or some of its member states.[29]

Of particular importance was the fourth point of the plan, which introduced the idea of compensation in relation to the issue of the Palestinian "right of return." And most important was the seventh point, which spoke of the "right of all countries in the region to live in peace." This formulation is virtually lifted out of Resolution 242 and was one of the central aspects of 242 that had prompted its total rejection by the PLO thirteen years earlier.

The Saudi plan was generally well received by the Arab countries with the exception of Syria. Inside Israel, the Begin government rejected it out of hand. But of considerable interest was the intense debate it provoked inside the PLO. Arafat was suspected of having participated in its drafting, and he made statements supportive of it. However, even within his own organization, Fatah, he found himself in a distinct minority. At the Arab summit the PLO pressed for the rejection of the plan and it was not taken up.

In the months following the rejection of the Fahd plan, the PLO-Israel ceasefire continued to hold tolerably well. But it became increasingly clear that key parties in Israel, such as Defense Minister Ariel Sharon and Chief of Staff Rafael Eitan, were pressuring for a full-scale invasion.[30] In June 1982, the Israeli ambassador to Britain was severely injured in an assassination attempt. Arafat denied that the PLO was responsible, but using the attack as a pretext, the Israelis launched their effort to wipe out the PLO once and for all.

From 1982 to the Present: Pursuit of Negotiations

In June 1982, the Israelis invaded Lebanon. Within days they reached Beirut. By the middle of August, a disengagement agreement had been negotiated, again through indirect means, and by the end of the month the PLO fighters evacuated Beirut. The PLO leadership established new headquarters in Tunis.

A large segment of the Israeli population opposed the invasion; in particular, there was strong opposition to proceeding beyond the forty kilometers originally announced as the limit to the Israeli advance. To many Israelis the invasion was the first "optional war." While the fighting continued, there were protests joined by as many as 50,000 participants. After the massacre of Palestinian civilians in Sabra and Shatila, an estimated 400,000 Israelis protested.

The strategy of armed struggle, identified in the Covenant as the only way of liberating Palestine, was always something of a myth. The Israeli invasion, which eliminated the PLO military presence in southern Lebanon, made continued belief in the myth all but impossible. One key result of the Lebanese war was that for the first time since 1967 PLO forces were no longer present in any area bordering Israel.

Even before the PLO evacuation from Beirut, Arafat accelerated his efforts to move toward a political settlement. Thus, on July 22, 1982, the PLO for the first time stated that it accepted the 1947 United Nations Partition Resolution, the very document cited in Israel's Declaration of Independence. And on July 25, 1982, Arafat stated his acceptance of all United Nations resolutions on the Palestinian question.[31] At the same time, the PLO refrained from explicitly saying that it accepted Resolution 242, and in an apparent contradiction of Arafat's statement that the PLO accepted all UN resolutions, the PNC would subsequently make clear the rejection of Resolution 242.

These ambiguities and contradictions continued to reflect the diversity of views within the PLO and Arafat's determination to lead the organization in new directions beyond the mythical consensus of the past.

On September 1, 1982, the day of the completion of the PLO evacuation from Beirut, President Reagan announced his plan for Middle East peace. From a Palestinian point of view the positive elements of the Reagan plan were that it:

–spoke of "the legitimate rights of the Palestinians";

–stated that "the United States will not support the use of any additional land for the purpose of settlements" during a proposed transition period;

–suggested an immediate settlement freeze;

–opposed Israeli sovereignty or permanent control over the West Bank and Gaza; and

–stated that the withdrawal provisions of 242 apply to all fronts, including the West Bank and Gaza.

The negative elements of the plan from a Palestinian point of view were that it:

–did not explicitly affirm a Palestinian right to self-determination;

–stated that "the United States will not support" the establishment of an independent Palestinian state, and instead proposes "self-government by the Palestinians of the West Bank and Gaza in association with Jordan"; and

–did not break any new ground with respect to recognition of the PLO.

The PLO initially adopted a cautious response to the Reagan plan. PLO leaders spoke well of certain aspects of it. A few days after President Reagan's speech the Arab League met in Fez, Morocco. This was to be a crucial decision point. The resolutions they adopted speak of the:

> Arab countries' determination to continue to work by all means for the establishment of peace based on justice in the Middle East and using the plan of President Habib Bourguiba, which is based on international legitimacy, as the foundation for solving the Palestinian question and the plan of His Majesty King Fahd ibn 'Abdul al-'Aziz. . . .[32]

The reference to Tunisian President Bourguiba's plan as the

foundation for solving the Palestinian question is remarkable since Bourguiba's plan calls for accepting the two-state solution as proposed in the Partition Resolution of 1947.

The Fez Resolution then goes on to enumerate eight principles. These correspond almost identically to the eight principles of the Fahd plan, which unfortunately had not been adopted when it was offered a year before. Like the Fahd plan, the Fez principles called for compensation for those not exercising the right to return, a brief U.N.-supervised transition period, and guarantees of "peace for all states in the region."

Thus, the Arab League in Fez adopted the position that Arafat had supported a year earlier, but had not been able to persuade Fatah to accept. The acceptance of the Fez Resolutions caused a split in the PLO delegation, with representatives from the PFLP, the PFLP-GC (Popular Front for the Liberation of Palestine-General Command), and one of the Fatah representatives taking issue with the seventh principle that provided for peace guarantees for all states in the region, essentially quoting Resolution 242.

Shortly after the Fez summit Arafat began a period of intensive activity in conjunction with King Hussein. The objective was to see if it was possible to take advantage of the positive aspects of the Reagan plan and to develop a joint position facilitating participation in negotiations. Since a critical issue was the refusal of either the United States or Israel to accept the PLO as a negotiating partner, much attention centered around ways of constructing a joint Jordanian-Palestinian delegation that would be acceptable to all parties.

On December 14, 1982, the Joint Jordanian-Palestinian Committee, which had been conducting negotiations between the PLO and Jordan, issued a communique which stated:

> The two sides agreed to continue joint political moves on all levels and in conformity with the Fez Summit resolution . . .[33]

In January 1983, the divisions within the PLO widened. In particular the PFLP and the DFLP issued a statement denouncing not only the Reagan plan, but the Fez Resolutions, negotiations with Israel, rapprochement with Jordan, and contacts "with any Zionist party whatsoever." The last item was aimed specifically at Arafat, who was at that point participating for the first time in publicly announced meetings with Israeli peace activists.

In February 1983, the sixteenth PNC was convened in Algiers. The PNC supported Arafat by endorsing the Fez Resolutions, but the wording was very tepid:

> The PNC considers the resolutions of the Fez Summit as the minimum for political action by the Arab states which must be complemented by military action in all that it entails in order to redress the balance of power in favor of the struggle and Arab and Palestinian rights.[34]

In an effort to narrow the gap between the American position on an independent state (the Reagan plan spoke of self-government in association with Jordan), the PNC passed a resolution stating that:

> The PNC sees future relations with Jordan developing on the basis of a confederation between two independent states.[35]

Tepid or not, this was all the authorization Arafat required. Subsequent to the PNC meeting, he continued his negotiations with Hussein. Early in April, Arafat and Hussein agreed on the text of a joint communiqué which Arafat would put before his colleagues. This made positive reference to the Reagan plan and pledged that Jordan and the PLO would work together in a joint delegation.

Arafat was unable to gain PLO support for the communiqué as worded. Gresh reports that at least three amendments were requested: removal of any reference to the Reagan plan, assertion of the Palestinian right to self-determination, and insistence on high-level PLO representation in the joint delegation. Hussein refused these changes and went on television to announce the failure of the joint efforts. The same day, April 10, 1983, Issam Sartawi, the leading PLO advocate of negotiations with the Israelis, was assassinated by agents of Abu Nidal.

In considering Arafat's inability to obtain PLO support for the joint communiqué it is important not to lose sight of the larger context. The PNC had affirmed the Fez Resolutions, which embodied the Fahd plan and thus Resolution 242's implicit acceptance of Israel's right to exist; the principle of negotiations had been accepted; the PNC had endorsed the idea of confederation with Jordan; and even the idea of a joint delegation foundered not on the concept but on details of the composition. Thus, Arafat had succeeded in leading the PLO deeply into the effort to negotiate a settlement. All this was accomplished within an environment in which the Reagan administration refused to pressure the Shamir government to cease settlement activity, and in which the United States adhered to its policies of refusing to recognize the PLO.

The Hussein-Arafat effort in 1983 to settle on a joint delegation to represent the Palestinians in negotiations was to be repeated even more intensively in 1985. By 1984 the split in the PLO had become so deep that Arafat had been only barely able to convene the seventeenth PNC, which was boycotted by several PLO constituent organizations including both the PFLP and the DFLP.

On February 11, 1985, Arafat and Hussein signed an agreement that committed the PLO and Jordan to work together "towards the achievement of a peaceful and just settlement of the Middle East crisis."[37] This was a clear commitment to try to bring about negotiations.

The first principle read:

> Total withdrawal from the territories occupied in 1967 for comprehensive peace as established in United Nations Resolutions and Security Council Resolutions.[38]

This principle embodied the notion of the exchange of territory for peace. It is the basic idea of Resolution 242, and the reference to Security Council resolutions can only mean Resolutions 242 and 338.

The second principle read:

> Right of self-determination for the Palestinian people: Palestinians will exercise their inalienable right of self-determination when Jordanians and Palestinians will be able to do so within the context of the formation of the proposed federated Arab states of Jordan and Palestine.[39]

Like the similar statement at the sixteenth PNC, this principle tended to close the gap between the demand for an independent

Palestinian state and the Reagan Administration "preference" that the West Bank and Gaza be "associated" with Jordan. From the Palestinian point of view it was critical that this be understood as a confederation which would be undertaken by the two states, and not that Jordan would become a federation of sub-entities.

The fifth principle read:

> And on this basis, peace negotiations will be conducted under the auspices of an international conference in which the five permanent members of the Security Council and all the parties to the conflict will participate, including the Palestine Liberation Organization, the sole legitimate representative of the Palestinian people, within a joint (Jordanian-Palestinian) delegation.[40]

With this principle the PLO committed itself to participating in negotiations with Israel.

Thus, two years after the failure to articulate a common framework with Hussein for pursuing negotiations, Arafat was able to gain sufficient support within the PLO to proceed. The signing of this accord should have settled any doubts about whether there had been a total transformation of the PLO since the days of the Covenant. Moreover, the accord was not merely a statement of principles governing an approach to peace negotiations. Rather it was a framework within which the PLO and Jordan were to act jointly in an attempt to bring those negotiations about.

And thus major sustained efforts were made over the next year. Joint Jordanian-Palestinian delegations visited Arab and European capitals to gain support for this approach. But the critical effort involved winning U.S. acceptance. There were two key points of U.S. opposition. First, the Reagan Administration was opposed to an international conference, preferring instead direct talks mediated by the United States along the lines of Camp David. And second, the United States remained opposed to PLO participation in negotiations.

Ultimately, the United States agreed to an international conference that would serve as an umbrella for direct talks. On the issue of PLO participation, the United States finally responded to Hussein's entreaties by stating:

When it is clearly on the public record that the PLO has accepted Resolutions 242 and 338, is prepared to negotiate peace
with Israel, and has renounced terrorism, the United States accepts the fact that an invitation will be issued to the PLO to attend
an international conference.[41]

The key issue was whether the PLO would accept 242 and 338.
Hussein indicated in his February 19, 1986 speech that he
believed he had a commitment from the PLO that they would.
The PLO maintains that their commitment was tied not to an invitation to the conference but to a U.S. commitment to the principle of Palestinian self-determination.

In response to the U.S. statement on conditional willingness
to see the PLO invited to the international conference, the PLO
transmitted, through Hussein, three alternative proposals,
which have since been described as conditional acceptance of
242 and 338. Each of the three was complex.

The first stated that if the PLO was invited to attend an international conference,

then the PLO would agree to participate...on the basis of securing the legitimate rights of the Palestinian people including their
right to self-determination. . .and on the basis of implementing
UN and Security Council resolutions pertinent to the Palestine
question, including Resolutions 242 and 338.[42]

The second formulation stated that,

the PLO expresses its willingness to negotiate...on the basis of
the Jordanian Palestinian accord...and on the basis of UN resolutions pertaining to the Palestine question, including Security
Council Resolutions 242 and 338.[43]

The third formulation stated that,

on the basis of UN resolutions pertaining to the Palestine question and the Arab region, including Resolutions 242 and 338, the
PLO shall participate in the international peace conference. . . .
The participation of the PLO. . .shall be on the basis of securing
the legitimate rights of the Palestinian people, including their
right to self-determination. . . .[44]

The United States found all of these formulations inadequate.
It cited two reasons: first, that each of them links "acceptance" of
242 and 338 to other United Nations resolutions, and, second,
that the PLO was prepared to agree to all three formulations

only if the United States would "pledge to affirm the right of self-determination of the Palestinian people."[45]

Following this episode, Hussein announced that he was unable to coordinate politically with the PLO. The termination of the effort at cooperation is odd and has never been fully explained. Why exactly did it go the way it did? Why did Hussein break off at this point rather than permit further efforts and formulations? The answers to these questions are not yet clear.

A careful reading of the formulations the PLO offered shows that in no case do they simply say that they accept 242 and 338; each formulation merely states their willingness to participate in a conference on the basis of these and other U.N. resolutions. Since this is exactly what they had said they would do when they signed the Amman Accord (the only difference being that now they mentioned 242 and 338 by name), it is odd that they would have required a U.S. pledge to support Palestinian self-determination as a requirement for saying what they had in essence already said a year earlier. Probably this requirement reflected continuing debates and struggles within the PLO, and within a year Arafat was to drop the condition that the United States affirm self-determination.

In any event the breakdown of the Amman Accord made possible the reunification of the PLO at the eighteenth PNC meeting, held in Algiers in April 1987. The eighteenth PNC was reported in the Western press as a "hardline" meeting, but a review of the resolutions will show that this is not an adequate assessment.

The resolutions open with the words "based on the charter of the Palestine National Council" and then go on as usual to contradict that document. Resolution 5 states a continued rejection of Security Council Resolution 242, but characterizes it in a rather mild way as "an unsuitable basis for solving the Palestinian cause because it deals with the Palestinian question as one of refugees and ignores the inalienable national rights of the Palestinian people."[46]

Resolution 7 reaffirms the Fez Resolutions, and Resolution 8 states that the PNC:

supports the holding of an international conference within the framework of the UN and under the auspices and with the participation of the permanent member states of the Security Council and the parties concerned in the conflict in the area including the PLO on an equal footing with the other parties, and stresses the necessity for the international conference to have full powers.[47]

It should be noted that this resolution speaks of the PLO as participating on an equal footing, but did not adopt stronger language insisting that the PLO be represented in an independent delegation.

And finally, with respect to meetings with Israeli citizens, another contentious issue, the PNC endorsed "developing the relations with the Israeli democratic forces which support the Palestinian people's struggle against occupation. . . ."[48]

Thus, the eighteenth PNC did nothing to reverse the basic thrust of the PLO towards achieving a negotiated settlement along the lines of the two-state solution.

In December 1987, the Uprising began in the territories. Both prior to the Uprising and during it, Arafat continued to push for negotiations. His public statements during this period were ever more moderate in tone. Thus, on September 7, 1987, at a United Nations-sponsored meeting of non-governmental organizations in Geneva, Arafat stated:

We insist on convening this International Conference under the auspices of the United Nations and on the basis of international legality as well as of the international resolutions approved by the United Nations relevant to the Palestinian cause and the Middle East crisis, and the resolutions of the Security Council including Resolutions 242 and 338. . . .[49]

This statement is very similar to that which the PLO offered the U.S. State Department eighteen months earlier. It is believed to be the first time Arafat publicly stated an explicit willingness to negotiate on the basis of 242 and 338. Thus the PLO made this statement without obtaining any U.S. commitment to Palestinian self-determination, as it had previously demanded.

On September 10, 1987, *Yediot Aharonot,* Israel's largest newspaper, quoted Arafat as saying,

> When I want to participate in a Peace Conference it is not in order to talk there with the representatives of the Arab states–it is in order to speak with Israel. I want to negotiate with my enemies–the same enemies against whom I fought for many years–in order to reach a just and comprehensive peace. I hope that the Israeli leaders will listen to me. [50]

And on November 9, 1987, *The Jerusalem Post* quoted a message to the Israeli people from Arafat, in which he said:

> The people of Israel must be made to know that you can't simply eliminate five million Palestinians and ignore their national rights just like you can't get rid of Israel. We must strive for a just solution, for the good of both peoples, and live in peace.
>
> I am striving for a solution to the Israeli-Palestinian conflict. Failure to find such a solution could lead to a local war, which could well escalate into a world war and a nuclear holocaust that would wipe out the human race.
>
> The PLO accepts all the decisions of the UN concerning the conflict including Resolution 242, an acceptance which we have announced publicly at international conferences. The PLO perceives all these conditions as part of an all-inclusive package, which it accepts in toto, as opposed to the government of Israeli which accepts only one decision and rejects all the others.

Here Arafat was actually saying that the PLO accepts 242 and 338, a more direct statement than saying that it would participate in a conference based on 242 and 338.[51]

And on March 20, 1988, three months into the Uprising, *The Jerusalem Post* published a report of a press conference Arafat gave to its correspondent in Germany in which he stated that he was "ready to negotiate with the Israeli government in an international conference." He then went on to say, "Naturally that means recognition [of Israel]. Is that clear enough?" The same article reported that Arafat reiterated that the PLO accepts Resolutions 242 and 338 and that the proposal for a binational state for Palestine has long been shelved. [52]

From June 7 to 9, 1988, there was a summit meeting of the Arab League in Algiers. At that meeting, the PLO distributed to the Western press a packet of materials. One of the items in the packet was entitled, "PLO View–Prospects of a Palestinian-Israeli Settlement." The text did not indicate any specific author.

On June 22, 1988, *The New York Times* printed the text as an op-ed piece under the authorship of Bassam Abu Sharif, Yasser Arafat's press spokesman. The article stated:

> The Palestinians want...lasting peace and security for themselves and the Israelis because no one can build his own future on the ruins of another's.
>
> We see no way for any dispute to be settled without direct talks between the parties to that dispute and we feel that any settlement imposed by an outside power will not stand the test of time.
>
> The P.L.O. raison d'être is not the undoing of Israel but the salvation of the Palestinian people and their rights....
>
> The P.L.O. accepts Resolutions 242 and 338. What prevents it from saying so unconditionally is not what is in the resolutions but what is not in them: Neither resolution says anything about the national rights of the Palestinian people....[53]

Sharif's statement was clearly prepared with Arafat's approval. And the statement pulled together many things that Arafat himself had said in previous statements. What was truly new about the piece was its tone and style. It was clearly directed at a Jewish audience. It spoke of the Palestinians' "understanding of the Jewish people's centuries of suffering." More than any other document to have emerged from the PLO in the course of the conflict, the Sharif essay can be viewed as a first step toward reconciliation.

The statement was denounced by various minor Palestinian rejectionist groups, but also by the PFLP. And subsequently Sharif was denounced by Abu Iyad, whose role in Fatah is second only to Arafat himself. Israeli Prime Minister Shamir responded to this piece just as he had to the earlier statements by Arafat, characterizing them as "nothing new."

In a literal sense, Shamir was correct. The Abu Sharif statement communicated a clear desire to make peace with Israel based on the two-state solution. This was not new. Arafat had provided the Israeli government with numerous opportunities to open a process that would lead to mutual recognition and peace negotiations. Furthermore, almost all of Sharif's proposals had previously been articulated by Arafat. Moreover, there was "nothing new" in Shamir's determination to ignore these openings.

That the Sharif statement was attacked by PLO hard-liners and by rejectionist organizations outside the PLO was also not new. One might remember the call for mutual recognition that Said Hammami made in 1973. But there was one big difference. In 1973 the PLO was still committed to the destruction of Israel. In 1988 the PLO was committed to negotiations.

Twenty years ago it was the PLO that refused to negotiate with Israel. Today it is Israel that refuses to negotiate with the PLO. For both Shamir and Peres, the reason is the same. The PLO is seeking to establish an independent Palestinian state; they are opposed to that. This is the key fact to be remembered. Israel was created within a commitment to the two-state solution. Forty years ago the Arab world rejected that idea. Today the tables are turned. It is Israel that rejects the two-state solution, and thus rejects the only basis for a stable peace in the region.

What follows is a strategy for achieving that peace.

Notes: Chapter 1

[1] Yehuda Lukacs, ed., *Documents on the Israeli-Palestinian Conflict* (Cambridge: Cambridge University Press, 1984), p. 1.

[2] *Ibid.*, p. 139.

[3] *Ibid.*, p. 138.

[4] *Ibid.*, p. 139.

[5] *Ibid.*, p. 140.

[6] *Ibid.*, p. 141.

[7] *Ibid.*, p. 142.

[8] *Ibid.*, p. 140.

[9] *Ibid.*, p. 142.

[10] *Ibid.*, p. 140.

[11] As quoted in Alain Gresh, *The PLO: The Struggle Within* (London: Zed Books, 1985), p. 40. There are two books on the PLO which I have found particularly useful. One is the volume by Gresh and the other is Helena Cobban's, *The Palestinian Liberation Organization: People, Power and Politics* (Cambridge: Cambridge University Press, 1984).

[12] This point is made by Gresh.

[13] See Gresh, *op. cit.*, p. 44.

[14] As quoted in Gresh, *op. cit.*, p. 48.

[15] *Palestine and the PLO*, PLO London Office, (undated but appears to be 1986), p. 30.

[16] As quoted in Gresh, *op. cit.*, p. 105.

[17] As quoted in Gresh, *op. cit.*, p. 106.

[18] As quoted in Gresh, *op. cit.*, p. 108.

[19] Henry Kissinger, *Years of Upheaval*, (Boston: Little, Brown and Company, 1982), p. 503.

[20] As quoted by Gresh, *op. cit.*, p. 146.

[21] As quoted by Gresh, *op. cit.*, p. 148.

[22] Lukacs, *op. cit.*, p. 157.

[23] Lukacs, *op. cit.*, p. 157.

[24] Lukacs, *op. cit.*, pp. 163-165.

[25] Uri Avnery, *My Friend, the Enemy*, (Westport, Connecticut: Lawrence Hill and Company, 1986) p. 154.

[26] Lukacs, *op. cit.*, p. 23.

[27] Lukacs, *op. cit.*, p. 11.

[28] See Ron Young, *Missed Opportunities for Peace*, (Philadelphia: American Friends Service Committee, 1987).

[29] Lukacs, *op. cit.*, p. 236.

[30] See Ron Young, *op. cit.*

[31] As cited in Gresh, *op. cit.*, p. 230.

[32] Lukacs, *op. cit.*, p. 237.

[33] Lukacs, *op. cit.*, p. 238.

[34] Lukacs, *op. cit.*, p. 208.

[35] Lukacs, *op. cit.*, p. 208.

[36] Gresh, *op. cit.*, p. 235.

[37] As contained in Ron Young, *op. cit.*, p. 142.

[38] *Ibid.*, p. 142.

[39] *Ibid.*, p. 142.

[40] *Ibid.*, p. 142.

[41] As quoted in King Hussein's Address on Middle East Peace, reprinted in the *Journal of Palestine Studies*, Summer 1986, p. 228.

[42] *Ibid.*, p. 242.

[43] *Ibid.*, p. 242.

[44] *Ibid.*, p. 242.

[45] Exchange of letters between Congressman Lee Hamilton and Secretary George Shultz as reprinted in the *Journal of Palestine Studies*, vol. 61, Autumn 1986, p. 234.

[46] "PNC Resolutions," *Israel and Palestine*, May, 1987, p. 16.

[47] *Ibid.*, p. 16.

[48] *Ibid.*, p. 18.

[49] As quoted in *The Other Israel*, No. 28/29 November-December, 1987, p.3.

[50] *Ibid.*, p.3.

[51] *Ibid.*, p. 3.
[52] *The Jerusalem Post*, March 20, 1988.
[53] *The New York Times*, June 22, 1988, p. A27.

Chapter 2
TIME FOR A NEW STRATEGY

It is clear that the PLO has undergone a thoroughgoing transformation with respect to both objectives and tactics. Once committed to the elimination of the State of Israel as its goal and to
armed struggle as its means, it is today seeking negotiations
leading to the two-state solution.

This transformation came gradually. There was no specific
moment at which the PLO abandoned the objective of eliminating Israel and decided to seek negotiations. Even today, one will
look in vain for a clear statement from the Palestine National
Council which explicitly disclaims any objective of destroying
Israel. And while there are today very few PLO attacks on Israel,
and while the PLO has ruled out attacking Israeli representatives or forces outside of Israel itself, its rhetoric continues
to pay homage to armed struggle.[1]

The organizational style of the PLO has been to deny and minimize transformation. This impulse emerges not only from an effort to preserve a precarious unity within the Palestinian
resistance movement, but also because to admit radical change
means admitting either to being wrong in the first place, to being
defeated in major objectives, or to being overtaken by events.

Almost no Palestinians believe they were morally wrong in
rejecting partition in 1947. They saw the creation of a Jewish state
in Palestine as unjust. Most still do. The PLO was the Palestinian
embodiment of the effort to try to reverse the perceived injustice.

With respect to defeat, it was not the PLO that was defeated;
it was the Arab armies. The defeats were inflicted in 1948, in
1956, and most tellingly in 1967. The PLO came into existence

aware of these defeats, but believing that they could be reversed. This proved impossible.

Essentially, the PLO was overtaken by events. Given the original objective of preventing the consolidation and continuation of the State of Israel, it is doubtful that any Palestinian movement would have had the resources to accomplish this end. This would have been true regardless of tactics, and regardless of leadership, even if the movement had begun in the 1940s. When it emerged in the late 1960s, Israel was by then an established and powerful entity. Two decades later, this is evident to everyone.

The great transformation of the PLO springs essentially from the underlying military reality. No conceivable strategy for destroying Israel has more than the most minimal probability of success. All such strategies expose the Palestinians and Arab nations to the high probability of totally unacceptable levels of destruction.

And as for political strategies whereby the Israelis will voluntarily decide to trade their Jewish state for a binational state, the real issue is power. The Israelis could entertain some notion of federation with a Palestinian entity, but they will never allow the essential functions of defense and internal security to leave Jewish hands. This is not because of racism, and it is not because of any lack of idealism. Even today, there are more idealists in Israel than in most countries. The issue is simply a matter of history. In a world of nation-states, given the history of Jewish suffering when the Jews were a stateless people, they simply will not voluntarily take those risks.

These facts have been obvious at least since 1967. It is in virtue of these facts that the Arab countries accepted Resolution 242 as long ago as 1971.[2] And it was these facts which underlay the decision of the Arab League summit at Fez in 1982 to seek a negotiated peace with Israel.

Unfortunately, the Israelis have grown very attached to the West Bank and Gaza. Inside Israel there remain important differences between the Likud and the Labor Party, especially with respect to yielding territory for peace. But both are united in their antipathy to dealing with the PLO and both have minimized or even totally denied the reality of the Palestinian transformation. Unfortunately, the style of the PLO, a style that fails to take full political advantage of changes in the organization's goals and tactics, has played into the hands of its opponents.

This is not to say that there has been no public enunciation of fundamental changes by the PLO. As we have seen, they have provided successive Israeli (and American) governments with ample opportunities for opening a process of dialogue, mutual recognition, and negotiations. The U.S. and Israeli responses have made clear that neither the Israeli nor the American political leadership has ever been interested in promoting such a process. Or to put it more cautiously, no American or Israeli leader has ever been interested enough in such a process to take any appreciable political risk to bring it about.[3]

This conclusion has not been lost on the PLO. In my meetings with Arafat and other PLO leaders in June 1987, Arafat spoke disparagingly of American and Israeli leaders as mere politicians and not statesmen.[4] He maintained that because the Israelis lacked anyone of the stature of de Gaulle, who led France out of Algeria, the Palestinians would have to focus on affecting Israeli public opinion. And he has continued to make and authorize statements designed to influence the Israeli population, as well as the American Jewish community.

Regrettably, the barriers of ideology, distrust, fear, hatred, and short-sightedness on the Israeli side make this a formidable challenge. When combined with the limitations on the Palestinian side–their tendency to deny change, the continued factionalism within the PLO, the diversity of objectives, the inability to end all attacks on Israel, and the degree to which pride and dignity are associated with resisting unilateral concessions–it is unlikely that Arafat will succeed in transforming Israeli attitudes. If he had an Israeli partner willing to participate in a step-by-step process of transforming attitudes on both sides, it would be a different story. To proceed unilaterally, what is needed would be *at least* the Palestinian equivalent of Sadat's visit to Jerusalem; probably more would be necessary. Such events are rare in international relations.

The Palestinian Uprising which began in December 1987 was not the first instance of massive civilian resistance to Israeli rule in the West Bank and Gaza. A careful reading of the history shows that there have been many outbursts of resistance since 1967. But the recent insurrection was unprecedented in two important ways. First, it involved the entire population of the territories. It was not restricted to certain groups or regions. And second, the depth of commitment that it both expressed and generated was unlike anything that came before. The Uprising has unified the population of the territories, and for the younger generation, it has been the decisive event around which their identity has been formed.

In the spring of 1988, when one asked young Palestinians to explain how the Palestinian struggle would proceed from the Uprising to an independent state, they appeared to be somewhat at a loss. The response was typically that the Uprising will put pressure on the United States to force Israel into an international conference that will create an independent Palestinian state.

This scenario, which largely represented the existing strategy of the PLO, is terribly unlikely. For its fulfillment, two events must occur. First, Israel has to agree to participate in an international conference in which the PLO is represented. And second, that conference has to result in an Israeli agreement to create a Palestinian state on the West Bank and Gaza.

Thus far an enormous amount of effort has been directed toward simply getting the Israelis to agree to a conference. To date these efforts have failed; but it is possible that a conference will actually be convened, with PLO representation. What is totally unlikely is that in such a conference Israel will agree to a Palestinian state. And it is similarly unlikely that the United States will attempt to force such a state upon a resistant Israel. Indeed, it is not clear that the United States could succeed in that effort were it to try.

But what does this mean? After enormous exertion on the part of the Palestinians within the territories, they may reach their immediate objective of a conference. This achievement will occasion great expectations, expectations which will not be fulfilled. Instead there will be endless maneuvers and delays. There will be recesses and adjournments. There will be countless efforts to overcome obstacles, but in the end, deadlock.

It does not take much imagination to realize what will happen at that point. For the Palestinians, having gone through the long march, having invested so much in negotiations, the realization that Israel will not permit a Palestinian state will be deeply traumatic. Throughout the territories Palestinians will ask, "Where do we go from here?" The rejectionists, who will have condemned Arafat and the negotiations, will appear to have been vindicated.

Many Palestinians will succumb to despair, but a significant number will conclude that there is no other alternative than to make occupation a hell for the Israelis. There will be a major upsurge in violence. The discipline on not using guns will break down, and events will spiral toward disaster for the Palestinians and possibly for the Israelis as well.

Is there no alternative? Is there no third way to the two-state solution, one which relies neither on negotiations nor on armed struggle?

It is time to question the underlying premise of the negotiations strategy: that prior Israeli consent is necessary for a Palestinian state to emerge. Consider as an alternative how the Israelis themselves proceeded in creating their state. They neither sought nor obtained Arab or Palestinian permission to create a state. Following the United Nations Partition Resolution of 1947, they unilaterally declared the existence of the State of Israel. They sought and received worldwide recognition. And when their claim was challenged by Arab armies, they gained effective control of territory through force of arms.

The Palestinians can do something analogous. The crucial difference is that they cannot rely on arms to make the Israelis withdraw. But by drawing on political, economic, psychological, and moral forces they can nonetheless bring about an Israeli withdrawal.

Until the Uprising this was not possible. But the Uprising transformed the psyches of the 1.5 million Palestinians living in the West Bank and Gaza. It has created a situation in which a new strategy is possible.

The strategy presented here is properly thought of as a strategy for the two-state solution. It thus embodies a strategy for creating a Palestinian state, but it is essentially a plan for achieving peace in the Middle East. This is more than a rhetorical point. The strategy will succeed only if it is undertaken as a peace initiative. Undertaken in any other spirit, it may well be a prescription for disaster.

As a strategy for the two-state solution, it is more than a strategy for Palestinians. Although the Palestinians are the primary actors, it is a strategy for all who are concerned to bring about peace. Moreover, it is idle to imagine that this strategy will be adopted merely by virtue of its brilliance. From the Palestinian perspective, the key issue is: will it succeed? The conditions under which it will succeed can to a considerable extent be effected by non-Palestinians, especially by Israeli peace forces and by Israel's friends in the United States.

The text that follows details the central elements of the strategy. Thirteen elements are identified, but they can be thought of as falling into four groupings:

1. The Unilateral Declaration of Statehood and the creation of a provisional government

2. The Peace Initiative

3. Creating the sinews of the state

4. Motivating the Israelis to withdraw.

These elements are interactive. Many people have called for a Palestinian peace initiative. So long as it remains a resistance movement, the PLO will not be able to do what needs to be done. The unilateral declaration of statehood and the creation of a provisional government, will establish a political and psychological vantage point that will liberate the Palestinians from the tethers of the past. It will provide a new beginning that will allow them to replace a style that denies and minimizes the reality of change with one that initiates and takes full advantage of it.

A declaration of statehood would be empty if it were not the case that the Palestinians in the territories are ready to build the living structures of a new state and society. The Uprising has demonstrated this reality, and the declaration of statehood will strengthen the Uprising by expanding its time horizon and by placing it within a meaningful political and diplomatic framework. Thus the strategy integrates the role of the leadership in Tunis with that of the population in the territories.

Full statehood will ultimately require Israeli withdrawal. But Israeli withdrawal cannot be achieved with guns. The peace initiative, itself made possible by the declaration of statehood, will create forces inside and outside Israel that will ultimately bring about withdrawal and possibly negotiations between the two states.

The approach laid out here is bold. And it is not without risk. The claim I make for it is simply that it has a better chance of bringing peace to the Middle East than any of the alternatives.

Notes: Chapter 2

[1] In the Cairo Declaration on Terrorism of 1985 Arafat ruled out actions outside of Palestine. And in the course of the Uprising, lethal attacks on Israelis in the West Bank and Gaza were similarly ruled out. Thus, only Israel within the green line remained a target area.

[2] Hussein indicated in his January 1986 speech that Jordan had been active in the passage of 242 in 1967. Egypt made clear its acceptance of 242 in 1971 in response to a questionnaire submitted by United Nations Secretary General Jarring. See Lukacs, *op. cit,"* p. 2.

[3] A critical factor from the U.S. point of view as well as that of the Labor Party has been the continued belief that it was always possible to deal with Jordan as an alternative.

[4] I represented the Jewish Committee for Israeli-Palestinian Peace in these meetings between May 31 and June 7, 1987. They are discussed in Jerome Segal, "Arafat Assures American Jews Negotiated Peace Is Possible," *The Washington Report on Middle East Affairs*, Vol. VI, no. 5, September 1987, p. 1.

Chapter 3
THE ELEMENTS OF THE PLAN

The Unilateral Declaration of Statehood

On May 14, 1948, a proclamation was issued in Tel Aviv. It read:

On November 29, 1947, the General Assembly of the United Nations adopted a Resolution for the establishment of an independent Jewish State in Palestine and called upon the inhabitants of the country to take such steps as may be necessary on their part to put the plan into effect.

This recognition by the United Nations of the right of the Jewish people to establish their independent State may not be revoked. It is, moreover, the self-evident right of the Jewish people to be a nation, as all other nations, in its own sovereign State.

ACCORDINGLY, WE, the members of the National Council, representing the Jewish people in Palestine and the Zionist movement of the world, met together in solemn assembly today, the day of termination of the British Mandate for Palestine, by virtue of the natural and historic right of the Jewish people and of the Resolution of the General Assembly of the United Nations,

HEREBY PROCLAIM the establishment of the Jewish State in Palestine, to be called ISRAEL.

We HEREBY DECLARE that as from the termination of the Mandate at midnight, this night of the 14th to 15th May, 1948 and until the setting up of the duly elected bodies of the State in accordance with a Constitution to be drawn up by a Constituent Assembly not later than the first day of October 1948, the present National Council shall act as the provisional administration, shall constitute the Provisional Government of the State of Israel. . . .

We offer peace and unity to all the neighboring states and their peoples, and invite them to cooperate with the independent Jewish nation for the common good of all.

An analogous declaration, the Declaration of the Existence of the State of Palestine, is the cornerstone on which the Palestinian state and, ultimately, peace in the Middle East will be based.

A declaration of statehood, under any circumstances, is a bold step. There are not many states in the world. They do not come into existence easily. To declare the existence of the State of Palestine under circumstances of Israeli military occupation will be one of the boldest acts imaginable. Yet, I will argue, to do so is the natural outgrowth of the Uprising itself. The Declaration of Statehood rests its logic on the actions of the 1.5 million Palestinians in the occupied territory. And it will be primarily their actions which will give meaning to that Declaration.

Given the fact of Israeli military occupation of the territories, one is likely to scoff at the idea of a Palestinian Declaration of Statehood. After all, the cat may look at himself in the mirror and solemnly tell himself that he is the king of the realm, yet this does not make him so.

In order to understand the logic of the unilateral declaration it is important to think through exactly what a state is, to understand how states come into existence, to grasp what it means for them to exist.

When we talk of states, we are talking of territorial states. A territorial state exists when there is a piece of territory over which some organization or individual claims sovereignty and when that claim is accepted by the people of that territory and by the other states of the world.

We can put this in a variety of alternative wordings. But essentially a territorial state exists when there is an entity which says, "I'm in charge. I make the rules about what goes on here." When the people inside the territory accede to the rule-making claim, and when other states do not effectively contest that claim, then a state has come into existence.

Thus the full existence of the State of Palestine in the West Bank and Gaza requires:

1. An entity that proclaims itself as the State of Palestine and as sovereign rule-maker over the territory.

2. Acceptance of that claim by the people of the territory.

3. The absence of any effective counter-claim.

When people accept a rule-giver they may do so for very different reasons. There may be an acceptance of the moral authority of that body, a recognition that the claimant has a *right* to rule (in virtue of having been chosen by the people, or in virtue of customs accepted by the people), or it might be a grudging acceptance by the people growing out of a generalized fear or unwillingness to contest the rule of the claimant. Most states in the world fall somewhere in between these two extremes.

Accepting the rule of a state is a general condition. It is not merely a matter of obeying an armed soldier when he stands in front of you and gives you a command. When a body rules, when a state exists, its laws are broadly obeyed and followed, even in the immediate absence of armed authority. Indeed, this is the typical mode of acceptance of rule, for it is impossible always to have a one-on-one confrontation between agents of the state and individual people.

Moreover, many of the rules of the state are simply procedures for doing things. The state says, "These are the conventions we will employ here." This power of the state, its power over conventions, is absolutely critical. Much of what we do in social life we do by virtue of a set of conventions accepted in the society. For instance, if two people stand in front of a certain figure and in accord with specific conventions, say certain words, that *counts* as their having gotten married. If one person signs a piece of paper, according to certain conventions, this may or may not count as his having signed a check or entered into a contract. It is the state that specifies those conventions and says what will count as what. The state can take a piece of paper, and print the words "Five Dollars" on it, and lo and behold, that piece of paper counts as money. Lo and behold, everyone in that society will do things in order to get that piece of paper.

Should everyone reject the state's rule, that is, reject the power of the state to set conventions, then what was money becomes paper, what was a marriage ceremony becomes empty words, what was a contract becomes a mere promise.

The question of whether or not a given state exists arises when there is an actual challenge to its rule in the territory over which it claims to be sovereign. Some other entity says "No"; it says "You are not in control"; it says, instead, "I am in control." And when it makes the claim stick, that is, when it in fact gains control over all the territory of the other state, then that first state ceases to exist. At that point, the king is reduced to merely being the cat in front of the mirror.

The loss of control and the ending of the existence of a state may be a matter of highly formalized symbolism, as when an emperor removes his crown or signs a document of unconditional surrender, or it may occur without any formal statement at all; it may just happen, even slowly over a long period of time. The state may fade away like water evaporating in the sunlight.

Consider the idea of a state gaining effective control over territory. This seems a simple enough concept, yet what exactly is it to gain control over a territory, especially when control is being contested? It cannot be a matter of physically occupying every square inch of a territory, as if control of a territory were something like having a piece of earth in a box, or a chestnut in one's pocket. States do not control territory in this way. To gain control of a territory is essentially to gain control not over the physical land itself, but over any people that occupy that land. Sometimes this can be done by removing or killing all the people there, or all those whom one cannot control. But if this route is not taken, then to control a territory is to gain the obedience of its people. Ultimately, it is to gain the acceptance by the people of one's rule-making authority.

In all this, one tremendously important point should now be obvious. The existence of a state is essentially a matter of the acceptance of its existence as a state by human beings. States are social inventions, political constructs. They are not physical entities. They cannot be detected by chemical tests or seen under microscopes. Their existence is dependent upon the attitudes and behavior of people. This is not to say that the body laying a claim to be a state or to be the governing body of a state ceases to exist merely because it is not accepted as such by the people. Rather its status changes. Once deposed by the people, either overtly or through collective disobedience and disregard, what was once the government of the state is now a band of individuals. Even if they have guns and weapons, if their ability to control is limited to the moments when they have someone at gun point, they are not a government. They are brigands, or criminals, or outlaws, or just foreign soldiers. But they are not a state.

The implications to be drawn for Israeli rule over the occupied territories are obvious. The strategy of disobedience and disregard already means that the Israelis have lost effective control of the territories. But at the moment, my concern is not with the Israelis and their effective control. It is with the other side of this political equation, with what it would be for a Palestinian state to come into existence, and why it is not folly to declare its existence even as the Israeli military occupation continues.

When a territorial state exists, it exercises its control over more than a piece of territory and the people within it. It exercises its control over its citizens, and these may either be inside the territory controlled or outside. If a state regards you as a citizen, it typically does not relinquish its claim to control and regulate what you do even if you are outside its territory. Thus, Americans who spend their lives almost totally abroad can still be required to pay U.S. taxes, to serve in the U.S. Army if there is a draft, and to obey American laws, (which sometimes apply to the conduct of Americans living in other countries).

Furthermore, though many states provide for practices whereby an individual may renounce his or her citizenship, these vary considerably, and it is perfectly possible to have states that do not allow citizenship to be relinquished. Moreover, these mechanisms of rights and obligations may extend to several generations. Thus, Switzerland is prepared to regard as a citizen any child of a male Swiss citizen, even if the father has himself never resided in Switzerland. In principle this may go on indefinitely.

The Unilateral Declaration of Statehood of the new State of Palestine will essentially be the establishment of a formal relationship between the people of Palestine and the entity that they accept as their government. Because the State of Palestine will have no significant power to coerce obedience from the Palestinian people, it will be, of necessity, a very particular kind of state: it will be a state whose very existence will depend on the free consent of the people themselves.

This point cannot be over-emphasized, for it means that there is in fact a great advantage both to the Palestinians and (as we shall argue) to regional peace, in having the State of Palestine come into existence at a time when the Israeli occupation continues. This will ensure that the State of Palestine will be a democracy (in the sense of its resting on the consent of the governed). Thus, not only is it possible to bring a state into existence in this manner, but it is the best way to create the State of Palestine.

The plan calls for a unilateral declaration to be issued simultaneously within the territories and from the outside. The declaration will be issued by the PLO as its final act. In the declaration, the PLO will proclaim the existence of the new state, and then itself go out of existence, to be superceded by the provisional government of the new state.[1]

Following the lines of the Israeli Declaration of Independence, the Palestinian Declaration might announce:

> We the members of the Palestine National Council (PNC) by virtue of the historic and natural right of the Palestinian people to be a nation, as all other nations, in its own sovereign state, hereby proclaim the establishment of the Palestinian state, to be known as Palestine.

> We further declare that the State of Palestine offers peace to all its neighboring states and looks forward to mutual cooperation for the common good of all.

Indeed, though this would be a point for serious exploration, the Palestinian Declaration could appeal to exactly the same international authority that the Israelis appealed to in their Declaration: the 1947 Partition Resolution of the United Nations. If they chose to do this, the Palestinians would be arguing that there is no statute of limitation on the Resolution, and that while they rejected it in 1947 they are accepting it now.

The implications of citing the Partition Resolution in the Palestinian Declaration would be powerful indeed. On one level, it would mean that the Palestinians were tying their legitimacy to the very same document that provides legitimacy for Israel and is cited in the Israeli Declaration. They would be taking the world back to common sense: the decision to solve the Arab-Israeli dispute through the establishment of two states, one Jewish, the other Palestinian.

In so doing, the Palestinians would be accepting the legitimacy of the state of Israel. To connect its Declaration of Statehood formally with the resolution providing for a Jewish state would be in a deeply symbolic manner to connect the existence of the State of Palestine with the continued right to exist of the State of Israel. It would be saying, "Our right to exist and your right to exist are mutually dependent."

The risk of such a move is that it probably would not be interpreted in this manner. It would be associated with and might actually precipitate a claim to all the territory that was supposed to be part of the Arab state as originally envisioned by the United Nations. Since this includes areas that have been part of Israel since 1948, and since it goes well beyond Resolution 242 (which essentially spoke of returning to the borders prior to the 1967 war), it might lead the Palestinians to make claims that could never be satisfied. It would also deepen Israeli suspicions of ultimate Palestinian willingness to settle for a state on the West Bank and Gaza.

All things considered, it would probably be best not to emphasize the Partition Resolution unless this was very clearly coupled with an assertion of sovereignty only over the West Bank and the Gaza Strip.

The Provisional Government

The Plan calls for the PLO, as the sole legitimate representative of the Palestinian people, to proclaim the existence of the State of Palestine and to establish the provisional government of the new state.

But what would this government consist of? The new

government could be set up as a tripartite government, consisting of an executive branch, a legislative branch, and a judiciary. At present, the PLO structure already includes an executive committee (Yasser Arafat is the Chairman of the Executive Committee of the PLO) and a legislative organ (the Palestine National Council (PNC)). Accordingly, the executive committee of the PLO would be transformed into the central decision-making unit of the executive branch. Exactly how it would function need not be spelled out here. By and large, it would be something like a cabinet, possibly along the Israeli model, where the Prime Minister is the first among equals, rather than the American model, in which all of the cabinet secretaries are presidential appointees.

Under these circumstances, there should be some increased devolution of power toward the legislative body, making it a more substantial organ than the PNC is at present. At the outset, it would be logical for executive and legislative positions to be occupied by many of the same individuals who now hold positions in the executive committee and the PNC. Over time, the new state would have to work out its processes for determining who will occupy which offices. As elections will not be possible within the territories until Israeli withdrawal, all positions, including that of President or Prime Minister, would be held provisionally.

One of the great advantages of replacing the PLO with a provisional government is that the Palestinians would get a new start. For instance, the PLO Covenant, which has been such a sticking point and which the PLO has always been very reluctant to amend, would simply be relegated to history. It would become an artifact, the covenant of a now defunct organization. The new government would be governed by a new constitution, one based on present realities, not on the fantasy of destroying Israel.

Because of the enormous symbolic importance attached to founding documents, and because of the history of the Covenant, the new constitution would have to be drafted with great care. It must not repeat any of those aspects of the Covenant associated with permanent and total rejection of the

State of Israel. This new constitution will be scrutinized thoroughly both by people inside Israel and those outside. It must clearly set the Palestinians on a new course, one that firmly espouses their commitment to live at peace with Israel within the framework of the two-state solution.

The provisional government should also provide for a judiciary. It is not necessary to wait for Israeli withdrawal before this body can begin functioning. Some citizens of the new state, who are living outside of the West Bank and Gaza, will be able to bring cases before the Palestinian courts. Ways might be found for matters concerning people inside the territories to be decided by the courts. Thus in interpreting statutes passed by the legislature, the judicial organs will no doubt, early on, have to decide how these bear upon people within the territories. In doing so, they will be extending the authority of the provisional government into the occupied land itself.

This raises a critical point. I have spoken of a provisional government, rather than a government-in-exile. What is the difference? The differences are two. First, the notion of a provisional government carries with it the explicit designation of its temporary composition. By design, the individuals holding state power are not intended to do so indefinitely. At the first possible opportunity, they will be subject to a normal electoral process. The concept of a government-in-exile does not explicitly affirm this, though it may be intended.

Second, and this is the crucial difference, to call something a government-in-exile is to concede that it exists outside the claimed territory, not inside. This is what exile means. But the provisional government will increasingly operate inside the territory as well as outside. Individuals holding top leadership positions will, of course, have to remain outside until Israeli withdrawal is achieved. But at lower levels, government officials will be inside, just as the PLO is currently inside the territory. And, just as at present, their identity as government officials will have to be kept secret from the Israelis. And because there will be a functioning government, it makes sense to say that the state exists.

The form of government most suitable under conditions of

continued Israeli occupation is one that is highly decentralized, with a great deal of power wielded by the organs of local government. Thus, within each village, operating within the framework of the new government, there can arise secretly elected local councils and boards. Their role would be to carry out the normal functions of government, such as decision-making with respect to schools and local police.

The secret leadership of the Uprising would continue in place as the leadership on the ground. However, rather than being merely a secret committee, they would be representatives of the government. As such they could and would receive acceptance and obedience from the population. Whereas under present conditions, every act of public adherence to the calls of the underground leadership is an act of defiance, under the new structure, every time someone heeded the call of the underground structure, it would also be a reaffirmation of the very existence of the state.

On the international level, the shift from PLO to provisional government would mean a symbolic upgrading of the position of PLO representatives. They would move from being representatives to being ambassadors. PLO offices would become embassies, and the Palestinian flag would fly above them as the emblem of a new country.

Finally, the creation of a provisional government will put an end to the fruitless efforts of those who seek to create a leadership for the Palestinian people. Both within the territories and internationally, virtually all Palestinians will accept the provisional government as the government of their state. At that point it will no longer matter whether or not a given individual or faction supports this or that policy of the state. Negotiations and agreements will have to be reached between the two states; this can occur only on a government-to-government level. Similarly, inside the territories, because the Palestinians will rally to the Declaration of Statehood, the decisions of the provisional government will be experienced as legally binding on all Palestinian citizens of the state.

This will cut two ways. On the one hand, the new government will have a greater authority than that attained by the PLO.

The average person will seek to be a law-abiding citizen of the new state of Palestine. If the government passes a law forbidding citizens to work for the Israeli military authorities, average Palestinians will obey because to do otherwise would be to divorce oneself from the ordinary ties between government and citizen. On the other hand, the actions of the government, more than ever, will have to reflect the views and attitudes of the public. Given the continued presence of the Israeli military, the Palestinian state will lack normal powers of ensuring obedience. And if it gets significantly out of touch with the people inside the territories, it will be disregarded, which in the case of the fledgling state means that it will in fact cease to exist. In short, the shift from PLO to provisional government will mean a significant leap forward in the mutual bonds and dependence between the leadership and the broad population.

Demilitarization and Unilateral Peace

The new government should immediately issue a proclamation declaring itself at peace with the State of Israel. Then it should announce that the State of Palestine will not maintain an army. These two provisions, a unilateral declaration of peace and a self-imposed demilitarization are closely related. They serve as essential parts not only of the process of winning worldwide support and eventual Israeli withdrawal, but also as critical components of the structure that will be needed over the long run to preserve peace in the region.

At bottom these two provisions carry one common message: the State of Palestine is not a threat to anyone. This message is verbalized in the declaration of peace with Israel, and it is made real by the decision that the state will not maintain an army.

Clearly these will not be easy steps to take. Several obstacles stand in the way. The first is pride. Why, one might ask, should the State of Palestine handcuff itself? Secondly, what reason is there to believe that it will be able to secure Israeli withdrawal through peaceful means, and why should it restrict itself unnecessarily? Furthermore, how in the future will the state be able to protect itself? If it has no army, how will it prevent invasion or domination by Israel or Jordan or Syria?

In addition to these questions, all of which must be answered, a very different problem arises: if in word and deed the State of Palestine is not a threat to anyone, this means that it has abandoned any long-term aspiration to wage war and destroy Israel. Are the Palestinians prepared not only to say this, but to structure their new state in such a manner that war against Israel becomes an impossibility?

The latter problem is the most fundamental. If it is not overcome, this entire strategy is worthless. Indeed, it may be worse than worthless, it may in fact be quite dangerous.

Ultimately, this is a plan for a peaceful and just resolution of the Israeli-Palestinian conflict within the two-state concept. The plan articulates a method whereby the Palestinian people, acting without the permission of Israel, the superpowers, or the Arab states, can take their destiny into their own hands and create an independent state. If this analysis is correct, then this plan is a possible means to the de facto imposition of the two-state solution.

At the same time, there are those who might be attracted to these ideas as a vehicle for creating a Palestinian state and then rejecting the two-state solution. Instead, it may be thought that a new Palestinian state could be used as a base for waging war against and ultimately destroying Israel. In short, it might be imagined that the strategy described here can be used for very different purposes than those intended.

I say "imagined" advisedly; indeed, the correct term might be "fantasized." Admittedly, most of the fantasies along these lines will be generated by Israelis, both by truly fearful people and by propagandists and ideologues seeking to retain Israeli control of the territory.

It is necessary to be very clear on three points:

1. It simply is impossible for a Palestinian state to someday be a base for a successful effort to destroy Israel.

2. If such fantasies are entertained by a significant portion of the Palestinian leadership, this will undermine the viability of

the strategy and prevent the full emergence of a Palestinian state.

3. Any effort to pursue such fantasies, to use the ideas in this strategy as a vehicle for aggression against Israel, will not only prevent the emergence of the Palestinian state, but will bring unprecedented disaster upon the Palestinian people.

The reason that a Palestinian effort to destroy Israel would fail should be obvious. The Israelis are an extremely security-conscious people. They possess the most advanced military technologies in the world. They have shown themselves to be among the world's best fighting forces. Virtually the entire population, including the women, has undergone military training. Adult males regularly serve extended periods of military service well into middle age. Time and again the Israelis have shown themselves to be prepared to take bold military steps without waiting for world permission and in the face of universal or near universal condemnation. The Israelis have an extended history of preemptive strikes. They have demonstrated no hesitancy in demolishing entire Arab villages, and in inducing vast exoduses of the Arab population. A major stream of thought in Israel provides ideological support for the belief that the territories, by right, belong to the Israelis. And certainly all Israelis would agree that if the Palestinian state were to evolve into a threat to Israel's existence, it would be the right and duty of the Israeli government to do whatever was necessary to block this threat, including either the evacuation of the entire area or the wholesale use of military force against civilian populations.

Israel is backed by the United States, and U.S. support can be expected to continue indefinitely. Furthermore, the Arab nations have never shown themselves willing to sacrifice their vital interests in a showdown struggle with Israel on behalf of the Palestinians. Indeed, a Palestinian state that took over Israel (á la the fantasy) would also pose a threat to both Jordan and Syria. In addition, since 1948 the Soviet Union has affirmed the legitimacy of Israel's existence, and it is committed to the two-state solution. Add to this the fact that Israel has a Jewish population twice the size of the present Palestinian population on the West Bank and Gaza and a vastly wealthier economy.

Finally, if anything more need be said, take note that Israel possesses a significant arsenal of nuclear weapons and would clearly use them against Arab armies if it felt it had to.

Surely, if anything in international affairs is demonstrable, it is that a Palestinian state in the West Bank and Gaza could not successfully wage a war of elimination against Israel.

Anyone who still harbors doubts about this is beyond the reach of rational considerations. Unfortunately there are many such people. Most of them are Jews. Indeed, in my experience, the only knowledgeable people who seem to treat such fanciful scenarios as serious possibilities are Jews. This terrible fearfulness is, of course, understandable. Jewish history, especially the reality of being abandoned by the entire world and subject to planned systematic annihilation by one of the most advanced and "civilized" of human societies, can be expected to blur the lines between what is and is not possible. It will take many, many generations before Jewish consciousness will recover from the terrible damage it still suffers at the hands of the Nazis.

Jewish fears, even irrational fears, are a fact. And for the Palestinians, they are a very crucial national security fact, which must take its place alongside the more tangible realities itemized above. For the fact of Jewish fear, when combined with the realities of overwhelming Israeli military power and prowess, guarantees that, if the project of building a Palestinian state becomes part of a project of destroying Israel, not only will it fail, blocked by unilateral Israeli military moves, but the catastrophe associated with this conflict will rise to a level far, far beyond anything that has yet been experienced in the Middle East.

And let us not hear anything about how the Palestinians might be out to trick the Israelis, first to create a peaceful state, to declare demilitarization, and then to build up the economy, slowly to rearm, and then someday to strike. No people in the world are less likely to be fooled on this score than the Israelis. Indeed, the real problem the Palestinians face is that even if their state is completely dedicated to peaceful existence with the Israelis, it may be impossible to convince the Israelis of this.

All of this leads to one very basic conclusion: *There can be no*

Palestinian state unless it is truly and deeply prepared from the outset to live at peace with Israel.

In order for there to be a Palestinian state, psychologically powerful means have to be found for convincing the Israelis of its peaceful intent. At the very least, because convincing the Israelis may simply be impossible given the depth of Israeli fear and suspicion, a means must be found for limiting the expression of these fears. The pragmatic elements that contribute positively to the Israeli political and psychological reality must be bolstered by the Palestinians. The Palestinian strategy must speak to Israeli fears and irrationality. Palestinians may find this requirement outrageous in view of their own weakness and suffering. They may quite understandably say that they are sick of hearing about Israeli fears and insecurities. But as understandable as this reaction may be, it does not change the facts.[2]

If someone raises the issue of pride and says that no self-respecting government can unilaterally agree not to have an army, the answer is this: If as a parent you find yourself and your children in a small room with a heavily armed crazy person, your obligation is to find a way of calming that crazy person, of taking his finger off the trigger. If you do not, you will never get your family out alive. There is no loss of pride involved in acting responsibly, for you are not dealing with an ordinary adversary. You are dealing with someone who must be treated not attacked. He is unstable and very dangerous. The Palestinians face an analogous situation.

Thus, I come back to this element of the plan: that as its very first act, the new government should declare itself at peace with Israel and should announce that the State of Palestine will not maintain an army. These steps will not be sufficient to quell Israeli suspicions, but they will be a very good beginning.

They will be very helpful moreover, in winning the support of other nations and of many Americans, and as will be discussed later on, this worldwide support will be instrumental in securing Israeli military withdrawal.

The answer to some of the other concerns I mentioned earlier should be now obvious. The Palestinians must demilitarize because it is the only way they will achieve their state. To pursue a military or guerrilla alternative is to invite almost certain suicide. Demilitarization is the State of Palestine's best defense policy.

How can an unarmed Palestinian state defend itself against Israel, Jordan, and Syria? Against Israel there is no defense. The Palestinians will have to accept "Finlandization," something that has not proved bad for the Finns.

With respect to Jordan, if the State of Palestine is no threat to Jordan, Jordan will be no threat to it. The reason is clear. If Jordan were to swallow Palestine, it would discover that the Palestinians had swallowed Jordan. Even today the Jordanian population is over 60 percent Palestinian. The only hope for the continued survival of the Hashemite dynasty as rulers in Jordan is for Palestinian nationalism to find its major expression elsewhere than in Jordan. There is only one place: the new State of Palestine.

And with respect to Syria, a look at the map will show that Syria will not border the new state. The new state will be a small enclave totally surrounded by Israel on the one side and Jordan on the other. Moreover, if Syria ever moved to take over such a state, either by invasion or subversion, this would clearly threaten Israel, and it would be Israeli national security interests that would maintain Palestinian independence against Syrian pressure. Indeed, this is exactly the role Israel now plays with respect to any possible moves by Syrian forces against Jordan.

In relying on outside powers for some of its national security needs, the State of Palestine will not be unique. There are other countries that by law, by constitutional provision, or by treaty do not have armed forces. For instance, Costa Rica by its constitution does not have an army. And it is the most prosperous of the Central American nations, a democracy that has avoided not only war with its neighbors but the internal civil wars and revolutions that are costing other Central American nations so dearly.

The unilateral declaration of peace and the affirmation of a demilitarized future, when viewed as part of the struggle for statehood, are an extension of the decision made by the Uprising not to use guns against the Israeli soldiers. When carried out on the diplomatic level, they will be responded to on that level. They will remove from Israel any excuse for continued occupation.

Finally let me add that there is another way of looking at demilitarization. Armies have been a stable feature of human society for a long time. But it is clear that the challenge of the future is to find ways of living together without them. Demilitarization can itself be an aspect of national pride, a way of setting an example for all nations. It is for the Costa Ricans; it can be so for the Palestinians as well.

The Provisional Government Bans Terrorism

In one of its very first moves, the provisional government should pass a law strictly forbidding all acts of terrorism and should impose stiff penalties for the planning or actual initiation of terrorist activity. From its inception the Palestinian cause has been harmed by the terrorism issue. It is absolutely essential that the new state start off clean on this score.

A few points about terrorism in the Middle East context are in order.

–First of all, as former Israeli head of military intelligence Yehoshafat Harkabi has said, there has been a "terrorization of thought" about the Middle East. The issue of terrorism has assumed unreal proportions; it has dominated discussion and prevented clear thinking from an Israeli point of view about Israel's interests and well-being.

–Terrorism has never posed a major threat to the existence of Israel. The Israelis faced real threats when they were engaged in serious wars against serious armies, but terrorism has never represented a threat of this kind.

–The Israeli leadership itself contains individuals with terrorist backgrounds. For instance, Prime Minister Shamir was a leader of the Stern Gang.

–There have been more civilian deaths among Palestinians from Israeli actions, whether terrorist or otherwise, than anything one can say in reverse. In this conflict, the Palestinians, mostly innocent civilians, have been the primary victims.

–The issue of terrorism has been exploited to avoid talking about what is today the main issue: the denial of legitimate Palestinian rights.

–Finally, the whole discussion is shot through and through with double standards and hypocrisy.

This being said, it remains the case that the new Palestinian state must address the terrorism question head-on.

Let me start with a definition. There is no perfect definition of terrorism (it is hard to come up with a perfect definition of anything), but we do not need one. By and large the following seems to work fairly well. A terrorist act is an act which, as a way of achieving a political or military goal, purposely harms or endangers ordinary civilians.

Another way of defining something is by example. Here are some examples of terrorism: attacking civilians in airports, hijacking buses, taking civilian hostages, air attacks targeted on civilian populations, rolling barrel bombs down into crowded marketplaces. These are all fairly self-evident examples of terrorism, but let us not get sidetracked on the issue of definition. We can have a good working definition of the term, and for policy purposes, the Palestinian state should err on the side of definitions that include too much rather than too little.

In order to understand why it is essential that the issue of terrorism finally be put to rest, let me approach the terrorism question from a different angle. As is well known, one of the preconditions the United States set for negotiations with the PLO was that the PLO recognize Israel's right to exist. (And let me say immediately that I believe Israel's right to exist is as firm as that of any other state.) Yet this is actually a very strange condition to find in international relations. The United States could have required that the PLO announce a willingness to make a lasting peace with the State of Israel or that it explicitly abandon any aim of destroying Israel. And if the conditions had been phrased in these ways, we in the United States could have argued over whether such declarations should be preconditions for negotiations or the outcome of negotiations. But at least we would know what we were talking about.

But what exactly is the right to exist? Are we talking about a legal right or a moral right? Whose right is it? Is it the right of persons? Of a people? Or is it the right of states?

If it is a right of states, then does it mean the right of a state to come into existence? Or is it the right of a state to continue to exist once it is in existence? Is it different than a right to live in peace? Under what conditions does a state have that right? When does it gain that right? When does it lose that right?

The point is that when applied to a state "a right to exist" is an obscure notion. There is no established tradition in international law, moral thought or political philosophy that deals in depth with the right of existence when applied to states. It is an interesting notion, and one that philosophers can play with. But it is hard to understand why such an obscure term has found its way into international diplomacy and U.S. law. Yet, there is another way of looking at it that tells a great deal about what is going on and helps make clear why the terrorism question is so important.

Six million Jews died because their right to exist as individual human beings was challenged. Genocide denied to the Jewish people as a whole the right to exist. This fact remains a tearing wound in the consciousness of every Jew in the world. It is this right of individual persons to exist and of a people to exist which is the deep psychological grounding of talk about a state's having a right to exist.

The Jewish people were the preeminently historical people of the ancient world. No other ancient people placed such emphasis on their own history and defined themselves so thoroughly in terms of their role in human history. Their understanding of history as unfolding, as meaningful, as a narrative with a specific direction, came to replace for Western civilization the Greek vision of history as cyclical. For contemporary Jews, the most widely observed holiday is Passover. And Passover is essentially an historical recounting of an episode in Jewish history in the Middle East over three thousand years ago. In recent decades many Jewish families have added to the Passover tradition a discussion of the Holocaust.

Whatever the Jews suffered in ancient Egypt, whatever left this indelible mark on Jewish consciousness for over three thousand years, cannot equal what has happened to the Jews in the twentieth century. Perhaps because we all know about the Holocaust and perhaps because it is so recent, we cannot fully grasp the fact that it was for Jews and for Western civilization one of the most important occurrences in all of history. It is part of the Jewish historical memory; for many still alive, it is part of their personal memory. And it will be part of the Jewish historical memory forever.

Now what is the relation of this to terrorism and the PLO? To some extent invocation of the Holocaust takes on a propagandistic dimension. Opposition to Zionism has been both deliberately and unconsciously conflated with opposition to Judaism. The Holocaust experience and the broader horror of Jewish experience under Christian rule has been simply projected onto the Middle Eastern context. But it is also true that the PLO has engaged in terrorism, and there is a vitally important symbolic connection between terrorism and the Holocaust.

Terrorism asserts the primacy of the project, of the struggle, of the cause over the everyday existence rights of ordinary people. It denies that there are any valid limits to how one wages a just fight or pursues a just cause. It says that all means are permissible. The renunciation of terrorism is a recognition that certain kinds of means are not allowed, even in a just struggle. This is analogous to designating certain actions war crimes, which is a way of saying that even in war some things are not permissible.

The terrorist purposely kills ordinary people, not for anything they have done, but because killing them is deemed useful. The terrorist refuses to recognize that ordinary people have a right to exist, which he is not morally permitted to violate even for a just cause.

For the remnants of a people who survived the Holocaust, terrorism is not a phony issue. For Jews inside and outside Israel, it reverberates with the most traumatic events in human history. On some level, especially for the most militant Israelis and American Jews, to fight the Palestinians is to fight all the historical enemies of the Jewish people. It is a tortured and convoluted way of trying to strike back at the Nazis.

Though many swaggering Israelis might deny it, Israeli foreign policy remains rooted in the experience of the Holocaust. For all that separates the Israeli soldier/citizen from American Jews who rarely serve in the armed forces, the common experience of Jewish history unites them powerfully. The slogan "never again" has, of course, been used as a moral blank check. Like the phrase "national security," it is invoked to suspend critical judgment, to justify any action of the state. But at the same time this concept of "never again" captures the ultimate essence of the Jewish will to survive in the post-Holocaust era. How else, accept around such a notion, could the remnants who survived have found the courage to function at all?

And because this notion of "never again" will continue to animate Jewish political action for decades and probably centuries to come, it is fruitless to look for simple parity. The Israelis may insist that the Palestinian state be at least partially demilitarized, but they will not demilitarize themselves. Whether or not this is fair, whether or not this is the best way to preserve Israeli security, this is simply the way it is. For the Palestinians, Jewish history is an ontological fact that must be dealt with; it cannot be wished away.

At bottom, for the average Israeli or American Jew, the association of the PLO with terrorism is so automatic that it is almost impossible to have a rational discussion of what, from an Israeli or American perspective, the most desirable policy toward the PLO should be. In some ways the Palestinians could not have found a more difficult adversary than the Jews of the late twentieth century, nor made a worse decision than to engage in terrorism.

In recent years, the PLO has made a significant effort to deal with this problem. In particular, in 1985, Arafat articulated a new PLO position in what came to be called *The Cairo Declaration on Terrorism*. It contains some basic advances that many people, even some well-versed in this issue, are not familiar with. First of all the Declaration issues a blanket condemnation of all acts of terrorism: "The PLO announces its criticism and condemnation of all acts of terrorism." Second, the Declaration signals the seriousness with which the PLO intended to approach the matter. It reads, "Beginning today, the PLO will take all measures to deter violators." This heralded that a real change was supposed to come with respect to implementation of the policy. Arafat was saying that the Declaration was more than a verbal renunciation; measures would be taken to enforce it. This commitment was critical for the renunciation to be credible.

The Declaration went on to assert that the Palestinian people have a right to resist occupation. This is a valid claim. But then, a very problematic turn was articulated. In speaking about the right to resist occupation, the Declaration asserted a right to resist "by all available means." With the insertion of the phrase "all available means," the Declaration becomes self-contradictory. Either all acts of terrorism are condemned, as the first part of the document says, or all available means are permissible in struggling against the occupation. The PLO cannot have it both ways. If all available means are permissible, then terrorism is permissible as a means of resistance. If all acts of terrorism are condemned, then some means are impermissible even when resisting occupation.

Then the Declaration takes an even more unfortunate turn. It says, ". . .events underline the certainty that terrorist operations committed outside Palestine hurt the cause of the Palestinian people." By making this point about terrorism outside Palestine, and failing to make a similar point about terrorism inside Palestine, the Declaration leaves itself open to the charge that it was condemning terrorism outside but condoning terrorism inside. Indeed, this is how the Declaration has been interpreted in Israel and in the United States. It is why the Declaration failed as an adequate renunciation of terrorism.

The PLO failure to correct the Cairo Declaration has been unfortunate. More important, of course, has been the failure to adhere to the blanket renunciation itself. The terrorism issue is not a card to be played. It is both a moral issue and an issue of common sense. Terrorism is not a help to the Palestinian cause. If anything has demonstrated this, it has been the Revolution of the Stones. It has been the decision not to employ guns in the West Bank and Gaza. It has been the demonstration that the tactics of struggle that are most removed from the taint of terrorism are the most successful.

The PLO position on terrorism has also been counterproductive in terms of PLO relations with the United States. It is now American law that no official or representative of the United States government may recognize or negotiate with the PLO or its representatives until the PLO accepts Security Council Resolutions 242 and 338, recognizes Israel's right to exist, and "renounces the use of terrorism." The law goes beyond the pledge made to Israel by former Secretary of State Kissinger in 1975. The Kissinger pledge dealt only with Resolutions 242 and 338 and Israel's right to exist. On the issue of terrorism it was silent.

There is a tendency to think that the terrorism issue is an excuse for a policy of denying the Palestinians a seat at the table. It is quite understandable that Palestinians would think this. First there is the simple fact of Israeli "dirty-hands." A Palestinian might ask, "How could it be possible that they really take such things seriously given what they have done to us?" And the terrorism issue has been used as an excuse. But it is a good deal more than that. It is a simple fact of life that there is a double standard in judging the morality of the actions of governments and of non-governments. Neither U.S. nor Israeli politicians created this double standard; it is part of the general hypocrisy that pervades the issue of morality and international relations. But it is a fact.

It would take a rare politician, whether Israeli or American, to have the courage to sit down with PLO representatives when the next day some terrorist attack on Israeli civilians might be broadcast across the world's TV screens. Thus, for instance, the attack on the Negev bus near Dimona in early 1988 was particularly self-defeating for Arafat's own diplomatic efforts to win acceptance of PLO participation in an international conference. Any politician who was considering support for negotiations with the PLO must have thanked his lucky stars that he or she had not spoken out.

The creation of a provisional government gives the Palestinians the opportunity of a fresh start. If it repeats the mistakes of the PLO with respect to terrorism, it will play into the hands of the Sharons and Kahanes who would like nothing better than to be able to utilize the full force of the military in dealing with "the Palestinian problem."

It is critical that the new government recognize that objectively the terrorist is the enemy of the Palestinian people and a danger to the Palestinian state. A leadership that cannot enforce a policy against terrorism or at least totally divorce itself from acts of terrorism will not lead the Palestinian people to self-determination. It simply will not happen.

The Exchange of Ambassadors and Mutual Recognition

One of the first acts of the new government should be to name its ambassador to Israel. Once named, an effort should be made to present credentials to the Israeli government and to establish an embassy inside Israel. Proceeding in this way will further reinforce the public commitment of the new government to the two-state solution. And it will answer the demands of those Israelis who ask, "How can you negotiate with someone who will not even recognize your right to exist?"

The effort to present credentials and gain acceptance of the Palestinian ambassador should not be carried out through the mail. Rather, the new ambassador should board a plane and fly to Israel, traveling on a new Palestinian passport. He or she will have to select an airline with some care, but hopefully he will find an American airline that will not refuse him passage. This can be ensured if the new ambassador is also a U.S. citizen.

Sending its ambassador to Israel will be an extraordinarily dramatic act. In some ways it will be even more dramatic than Sadat's visit to Jerusalem, because there will be a great question mark as to how the Israelis will respond.[3] What will they do? Will they refuse to let the ambassador leave the plane? Will they arrest him, thus violating standard protocols of diplomatic immunity? Or will they in fact allow him or her to enter? Will they extend an open, if skeptical, hand? The last alternative is not likely, but it is possible, and it will be supported by many Israelis and many in the Jewish community in the United States.

Once the state has been proclaimed, the notion of mutual recognition will take on a clear meaning. Until now, it has been a somewhat murky term, even though it is supported by many organizations. Just who is supposed to recognize whom? Is the PLO supposed to recognize Israel? And who or what is the Israeli government supposed to recognize? Are they supposed to recognize the Palestinian people? What does that mean? Or are they supposed to recognize the PLO? If the latter, what are they supposed to recognize the PLO as? Certainly not as the government of Palestine, for the PLO itself makes no such claim, and to date there is no State of Palestine. Once the state is proclaimed, all this simplifies considerably.

The selection of the Palestinian ambassador to Israel should be made with great care. For this individual will be both a spokesperson for his government and a symbol of Palestinian intentions. As with all ambassadorial appointments worldwide, it must be made with a sensitivity to the concerns of the host country. Thus, the Palestinian chosen will have to be both an individual of considerable stature and skill as well as someone with impeccable credentials. There is no shortage of such Palestinians. But it will be interesting to see who is named and how he or she carries himself.

At the same time, the new state should invite Israel to name an ambassador to Palestine. It is too much to imagine that they will do so in the short run. But at least the gesture should be made, the invitation extended. Israeli refusal will take on a much more serious aspect when it becomes clear that many other states are in fact naming their ambassadors to Palestine.

Where will such ambassadors go given that there is no territory under Palestinian control? One possibility is that they will go to Jerusalem and attempt to establish their embassies to Palestine right there. If they make this attempt, or if they attempt to set up in the West Bank or Gaza, it will confront the Israeli government with a delicate problem. The accumulation of such problems will bit by bit be the material out of which the seriousness of the Palestinian Declaration of Statehood will be constituted.

If the new ambassadors are prepared to go to Jerusalem, then these nations must also direct their ambassadors to Israel to go to Jerusalem. At present, almost all nations station their ambassador to Israel in Tel Aviv. The United States does so as well, though this may change. This is because almost no nation in the world recognizes the Israeli claim to sovereignty over Jerusalem, which was supposed to be an international city under the original United Nations Partition Resolution of 1947.

Probably the most interesting way to proceed would be for the ambassador to Israel from third countries to be named both ambassador to Israel and to Palestine. In that capacity, he or she should reside in Jerusalem, which both states will be claiming as their capital. The provisional government of Palestine should support this move. It should not lay any exclusive claim to Jerusalem, but instead argue that, with creativity, a way can be found to make that one city serve as the capital (i.e., seat of government) for both countries. To do so would be to take another step toward allaying Israeli fears that the Palestinians are really seeking to take over everything.

What will the Israelis do with respect to those states that name their current ambassadors to Israel as ambassadors to Palestine as well? Will they expel them, thus forcing themselves into deeper and deeper international isolation? Or will they quietly allow them to remain and perhaps move to Jerusalem, thus implicitly taking a step toward their own eventual recognition of the State of Palestine?

The provisional government should even go so far as to call on states that do not now have relations with Israel to name an ambassador to Israel and Palestine. In particular, the more hostile Arab states should be asked to do so. Thus, Israel would be offered something very attractive: by accepting an ambassador to Palestine, it would gain recognition of itself from an Arab country. The same goes for the Soviet Union and Eastern bloc nations that do not at present have embassies in Israel.

These symbolic acts are tremendously important. What they will symbolize is that Israel can, by accepting the reality of the State of Palestine, normalize its relations with all the states of the world. Israel will be offered the opportunity to end its global isolation, and when these offers come from the various Arab countries, and when they come at the urging of the provisional government of Palestine, the great benefit that the two-state solution holds for Israel will become increasingly apparent.

Worldwide Recognition and Admission to the United Nations

As soon as the new state is declared, it should seek recognition worldwide. Of course, Israel will be the last state to provide this recognition, and it is likely that the United States will be the next to last. But which nation will be first?

One possibility is the Soviet Union. The Soviet Union supported the Partition Resolution in 1947 and recognized Israel within seventy-two hours of the Declaration of Independence. It has never wavered in its support of the two-state solution. The unilateral Declaration of Statehood will put the Soviet Union in an interesting spot. Here, after years of having to accept the fact that all action in the Middle East depends on the United States, it will be confronted with a Palestinian initiative that at the same time will be extremely popular within the Third World, widely supported by the Arab masses, directed at an outcome that the Soviets have supported for forty years, and opposed by the United States. It is quite possible that under these circumstances, the Soviets will want to place themselves at the head of the list of nations providing recognition for the new state.

This prospect holds some dangers for the Palestinians. The most important is that it will tend to cast the issue of the Palestinian state into East-West terms, with the Soviets emerging as the great champion and the United States the great holdout. If the issue is cast in these terms, Israeli opponents of Palestinian statehood will be given an additional lever to use in waging their campaign of opposition. The new State of Palestine will be pictured as a new pro-Soviet state in the Middle East and one right next to Israel at that!

Palestinian diplomats will have to be alert to these problems. Perhaps efforts should be made in advance to restrain Soviet enthusiasm. In any event, the new state will have to make abundantly clear that it has no intention of getting involved in any aspect of superpower competition. Several important steps can be taken to make this clear. First of all, as we shall discuss below, the new state should be a democracy, and it should provide its citizens with a variety of protections of individual liberty. This the Palestinians will want to do for its own sake, but it will serve them well diplomatically. The new government might consider adopting a constitution. If so, there are considerable merits in the model that the U.S. Constitution provides. Diplomatically, this would be useful because by and large our own system is all that Americans understand and respect.

In the campaign for recognition a major effort should be launched in the United States. Ultimately, it is doubtful that the United States will adopt a policy opposed by Israel, but by winning popular support within the United States, especially within the American Jewish community, much can be accomplished that will be helpful in dealing with the Israelis.

One advantage of proclaiming the provisional government is that the legislative and policy obstacles to U.S. contact and negotiation with the PLO will be overcome. At present, by law as well as by policy, the United States has closed PLO offices on American territory with the exception of the PLO observer mission at the U.N., and U.S. diplomats are prevented from negotiating with the PLO. As mentioned earlier, any easing of these prohibitions has been tied to a variety of conditions: acceptance of Israel's right to exist, renunciation of terrorism, and acceptance of United Nations Resolutions 242 and 338. With the PLO no longer in existence, these restrictions can be expected to be applied to the provisional government, which many in the United States will designate as "the PLO in disguise."

However, the new government will in fact be able to meet all of the conditions imposed, and it can meet them with dignity, without having to jump through hoops held by the American Israeli Public Affairs Committee (AIPAC) or Henry Kissinger. With the PLO covenant no longer applicable, with the offer to exchange ambassadors with Israel, and with the unilateral declaration of peace, the State of Palestine will have satisfied the first condition: that it accepts Israel's right to exist. The renunciation of terrorism will satisfy the second condition. And the new state will be in a position to accept Resolution 242 unambiguously without any further mention of other United Nations resolutions.

Why do I say this with respect to Resolution 242? The answer is simple. The basic PLO objection to Resolution 242 is that it nowhere mentions the Palestinians except obliquely as a refugee problem. While affirming the right of all states in the region to live at peace, it says nothing about Palestinian rights. Not being in possession of a state, the Palestinians are left out of the resolution. But once the State of Palestine is proclaimed, the situation is quite different. Resolution 242 calls for respecting the rights of *all* states in the region. It mentions none by name, not Israel, not Egypt, not Syria, not Jordan. As one of the states in the region, the new State of Palestine should be able proudly to claim its right to live at peace within secure and recognized boundaries, as proclaimed by 242 and reinforced by 338. Once Palestine is a state, Palestinians will find that Resolution 242 provides them with exactly the policies they seek. It calls on Israel to withdraw from the West Bank and Gaza, and it calls for recognition of the rights of all states to live at peace.

Of course, U.S. policy is never purely a matter of logic. Domestic politics will remain central to these issues. But with the various peace initiatives outlined here, the new state of Palestine will receive widespread support within the United States, and most important, within the Jewish community. The splits that have recently divided the Jewish community will deepen, as many come to recognize the Palestinian initiative for what it is: an historic opportunity to bring peace to the Middle East on terms which make possible an Israel that is humane, secure, democratic, and a Jewish state.

Under these conditions, it could be expected that while the

United States will not officially recognize the State of Palestine, it will allow for the opening of offices of the new state and for regular contact between its representatives and those of the U.S. government. These contacts, as well as contacts with Jewish representatives in Congress, should be used to explore ways of mitigating American and Israeli fears. For the Palestinians, only so recently shut out from the American political scene with the closing of the PLO information office in Washington in 1987, it will represent the dawning of a new day.

The PLO already holds observer status at the United Nations. The new state should seek admission to the U.N. and to all other international bodies. With respect to the United Nations, this cannot be achieved without the agreement of the United States, for admission to the United Nations requires a two-thirds majority of the General Assembly, upon the recommendation of a majority of the Security Council, including all of the permanent members. In other words, the United States would have a veto.

This notwithstanding, the General Assembly can make recommendations to the Security Council on admission questions, and it has done so in the past. Thus, the new state should pursue initiatives in the General Assembly and in the special U.N. agencies. Regularly the Security Council should be asked to vote on recommending admission of the new state. If the United States continues to exercise its veto in the face of overwhelming worldwide support, this will be one more vehicle for motivating U.S. efforts to gain Israeli acceptance of the new state.

As far as the rest of the world is concerned, it is likely that almost all Third World countries will immediately recognize the new state. Thus, PLO offices everywhere will become embassies, and the leader of the State of Palestine will be elevated to the status of a head of state in the eyes of most of the world.

A particularly interesting arena will be the Western European countries. Their support is critical. Great Britain and France are members of the Security Council. As a group they are major trading partners with Israel. And as fellow democracies, their views carry some weight both in Israel and in the United States.

This differs from country to country, but, for instance, the Netherlands is highly respected in Israel–for her anti-Nazi past.

The Palestinian Uprising has already gained widespread sympathy for the Palestinians among Europeans, which has translated into a number of diplomatic victories. Early in 1988 the European Economic Community refused to go ahead with long-planned steps to grant trade advantages to Israel. Under these circumstances, it is highly likely that the Palestinian state will gain recognition from various Western nations once it makes its unilateral peace with Israel.

Negotiations, Boundaries, and Permanent Peace

Following on the offer to exchange ambassadors, the new state should launch its effort to begin negotiations. While I believe that Israeli recognition of the State of Palestine is not necessary, and that it is possible to make the state a full reality without Israeli concurrence, there would be great value in accomplishing this through negotiations.

Direct negotiations between representatives of the State of Israel and the State of Palestine would mean that some of the most basic issues had already been resolved. Specifically, the commencement of negotiations would mean mutual recognition by both states and would carry the clear message that peaceful coexistence was the goal of both sides. Thus, the very opening of such negotiations would be an unprecedented breakthrough, signaling that this seemingly impossible conflict was moving toward resolution.

Such negotiations between the two states would differ enormously from current proposals for an international conference at which Palestinians would be represented in a joint Jordanian-Palestinian delegation. Even if the PLO were somehow to be represented in its own right in such negotiations, and even if the Israelis could be induced to sit down with them, this arrangement would lack the far-reaching meaning of negotiations between the two states.

All that said, negotiations between the two states, were they to occur, would be long and difficult. The range of issues on the table would be vast indeed: final boundary lines between the two states; the status of Jerusalem; the status of the Israeli settlers on the West Bank; the right to return of Palestinian refugees from the 1948 and 1967 wars; demilitarization and Israeli withdrawal.

Given what we have seen of the negotiations between Israel and Egypt over Taba, a virtually meaningless pittance of land in the Sinai, one can seriously doubt that Israeli-Palestinian negotiations would ever resolve many of these issues. But there is a big difference between these negotiations and any others. While these negotiations continue, the two sides are at peace and have already accepted each other's existence as states.

Much could be said about each of the tremendously difficult issues to be negotiated, and in Chapter four I will address some pertinent questions. But it should be remembered that in one form or another the same issues confront any negotiated end to the conflict, regardless of whether it is achieved through the Shultz Plan, the present PLO option for an international conference, or some variant of what is proposed here.

Because Israeli willingness to negotiate with the leadership of the State of Palestine, would be so far-reaching in its implications, it is very unlikely that any Israeli government would, in the near future, agree to negotiate. These negotiations would mean acceptance of the two-state solution; they would be negotiations over how to make the two-state solution work, not over whether or not to have the two-state solution. Since both Peres and Shamir are adamant in their opposition to a Palestinian state, we can expect that they would refuse to negotiate with it. And there is no present Israeli leader who is waiting in the wings. Moreover, at present the Israeli public is at one in its rejection of any Palestinian state. So the opening of the kind of negotiations we are talking about will have to await broad changes within Israeli society.

These changes can occur, but they will take time and they will require that two facts become increasingly clear: 1) that a Palestinian state has indeed come into existence and that the costs to Israel of attempting to destroy it are unacceptable; and 2) that this state is seriously interested in making a permanent peace with Israel. When both of these facts are accepted within Israel, it will be possible and, indeed, essential to open negotiations. But it will be an uphill battle to convince Israelis on either score.

Nevertheless, the offer to open peace negotiations will be in itself useful. Within Israel it will strengthen the hand of the peace forces. It will be another demonstration of the real promise of peace that the two-state solution holds for Israel. It will provide further evidence that the new Palestinian state will not seek to destroy Israel.

And the offer to open negotiations will serve vital purposes on the international level. For non-Israelis, the Palestinian offer at direct negotiations and an initial Israeli refusal will carry a powerful message. It will show that it is the Israelis, not the Palestinians, who are standing in the way of a resolution of the conflict. This perception will itself play a major role in strengthening the hand of the new government as it turns toward ways of bringing about Israeli withdrawal without negotiations. And as indicated earlier, it will be the dawning awareness of the fact that the State of Palestine is becoming a concrete reality that will ultimately increase Israeli willingness to negotiate.

The Central Demand: Israeli Withdrawal

Assuming that the Israeli government rejects the Palestinian offer of direct negotiations, the situation becomes increasingly simplified. The Palestinian state has already been proclaimed. It is recognized around the world. It is affirmed by the Palestinian people. It has declared itself at peace with Israel. It has offered to negotiate boundaries. With the Israeli refusal, there is only one thing left: Israelis go home.

The creation of the State of Palestine transforms the status of the West Bank and Gaza. Until now they have been lands in limbo. Before 1948 they were under the British Mandate. Between 1948 and 1967 they were occupied by Jordan. Jordan made moves to annex them, but no country in the world recognized this annexation. In the 1967 war, the Israelis drove out the Jordanians but they have not claimed sovereignty. Thus, these are "the occupied territories." With the proclamation of the State of Palestine they are transformed from occupied territories into an occupied country.

By what right can the Israelis continue to occupy a foreign country? That is the question to be pressed in the campaign for withdrawal. The only legitimate basis for occupation is self-protection. But the Palestinian declaration of peace and offer to negotiate a formal peace treaty remove this excuse. The Israeli government will find itself in the untenable position of refusing to negotiate and refusing to withdraw.

The campaign for withdrawal is separate from the effort to secure Israeli recognition. The issue is not one of establishing formal relations between Israel and the State of Palestine. Israeli recognition is not a precondition for Israeli withdrawal. The United States continued to refuse recognition to what used to be referred to as "Red China" for some twenty years after the Communist forces gained effective control of that territory. Even today, some forty years after Israel came into being, it still is not recognized by most of its neighbors. The Palestinian state does not need Israeli recognition; what it needs is for the Israeli troops to go home.

This, of course, will be understood by any Israeli government. And most likely Israel will have a government determined to remain in the West Bank and Gaza. But the peace campaign and the offer of mutual recognition will have affected many Israelis. If they are not a majority, they will be an important part of Israeli society. The struggle for withdrawal is in many ways a struggle to help those Israelis save Israel from itself.

There is one school of thought that needs to be addressed immediately. The point is made that Israeli withdrawal from Lebanon was not caused by Sabra and Shatila, that Israeli withdrawal from the Sinai was not caused by Sadat's visit to Jerusalem, and that American withdrawal from Vietnam was not caused by youthful protestors. Rather, it is argued, withdrawal is brought about by body bags. One Israeli proponent of this view goes so far as to specify exactly how many Israeli deaths it will take to effect an Israeli withdrawal: two thousand.

On the basis of this view, the Israelis can be forced out of the West Bank and Gaza by a guerrilla campaign. For some this proposition is appealing. After all, war is so simple. It is clear-cut. You attack; you kill; you are killed. Victories and defeats are easily measured. And for some of the commando groups inside the PLO, this view has the great attraction of making their skills central to the cause of Palestinian liberation.

The Palestinian government will face no issue more fateful than its choice of *how* to wage the campaign for Israeli withdrawal. On this question rides the entire destiny of the Palestinian people.

First, the choice must be made clear. Sometimes it is put as a choice between violence and nonviolence. This is a close approximation, but it is not exactly correct. And the difference makes a difference. The choice is really between lethal means and non-lethal means. It is a choice between the "body-bags" strategy and everything else. Thus, stone-throwing, which has proved vitally important to the Uprising, is clearly a violent means, but it is largely non-lethal and has been carried out with a determination to keep the Palestinian side of the struggle non-lethal. The choice is really one of continuing with this decision to stick to non-lethal means (and enriching the variety of tactics and their effectiveness) *or* to abandon the non-lethal character of the Uprising and to seek to cause Israeli deaths.

The case for the non-lethal strategy is overwhelming. Its broad outlines are easily stated:

–A non-lethal strategy will achieve Israeli withdrawal with relatively few Palestinian casualties.

–A lethal strategy will not only fail to win withdrawal, it will result in the destruction of the new Palestinian state and it will bring staggering suffering to the Palestinians.

The alternatives are stark. Before explaining why, it is critical to understand the logic of the decision. In many ways it resembles "Pascal's Wager." Pascal, the great French philosopher and mathematician, considered the question of whether or not to believe in God. He argued that either God exists or he does not. Suppose he does. Then if I believe, the rewards are great (I go to Heaven) and if I do not, the costs are great (I go to hell). But if God does not exist, I have not lost much by believing or gained much by not believing. Thus since believing has potentially high gains and at worst low costs, and since not believing has at best low gains and potentially high costs, it is wise to believe.

The situation of the Palestinian people can be posed in similar terms. If the non-lethal strategy is tried and fails, it is always possible to try it again or to try something else. If the lethal strategy is tried and fails, all will be lost. Thus, even the proponents of the lethal strategy must recognize that they should not press their case. Only after all other alternatives are exhausted should a decision on the lethal strategy be taken. Whether the lethal strategy proves ultimately correct or not, *it is not what you do first*. At best, it is what you do last, or not at all.

In all instances, Israeli withdrawal will be secured not because the Israelis are physically forced out of the territories, but because they are forced out politically and psychologically. This holds even for the lethal strategy. A country with a population of over four million is not physically forced to withdraw by two thousand deaths. It is worth remembering that when they faced Roman legions, ancient Israeli policymakers "accepted" several hundred thousand deaths.

Thus, all relevant discussion centers on how best to affect the will of the Israelis. In some sense, they must be brought to want to leave. Now they will not want to leave because they have decided that it is the right thing to do, or because they have finally come to recognize the humanity of the Palestinians. Though these will be factors, and these attitudes will be held by a significant part of the Israeli public, just as they are by a minority now, they will never be the basic reason why the Israelis will "want" to leave. Essentially, all strategies are a matter of affecting the costs and benefits of alternative Israeli policies as they are perceived by Israeli decision-makers, and of affecting who comes to make the decisions inside Israel.

A non-lethal strategy can motivate Israeli withdrawal. On the benefit side, withdrawal holds out the real possibility for the Israelis that they will achieve their three basic aims: national security, Israel as a Jewish state, and Israel as a democracy. Israel faces insoluble problems if it does not withdraw. What can it do with the West Bank and Gaza? If it annexes the territories, then it must either institute apartheid or it must give the Palestinians the full rights of Israeli citizens. If it grants the latter, it will soon have a non-Jewish majority. Thus, Israel as Jewish and Israel as democratic are incompatible so long as Israel holds the territories. I say "holds" because this problem really exists whether Israel annexes or not. The issue of Israeli democracy is not something that arises in the future; it is an issue in the present. However, if Israel annexes the territories, then the issue of democracy will emerge from the closet. It will shift from being a moral issue of little concern to many, to being a political issue of considerable urgency to the Israelis themselves.

If Israel attempts some radical solution such as expelling the Palestinians, it will discover that they will not go. It will not be like 1948 when the population could be panicked into mass exodus. In every village, in every city, Israeli troops will have to kill large numbers of Palestinians who will have decided to take a last stand. Such a move will probably trigger another war with the Arab states, and even if it did not, it runs the risk of triggering a revolution in Jordan and the takeover of Jordan by the PLO, with the prospect of never-ending war and instability.

So Israel has major national security problems unless it achieves a just peace with the Palestinians. The non-lethal strategy has the great benefit of offering the Israelis a solution to their most central problems, a solution, moreover, that they can afford to take. Because they will have retained the fighting morale of the army, they can always argue that if things do not work out, they can reoccupy. Indeed, from the Israeli point of view, withdrawal not accompanied by recognition can be portrayed as conditional, as a test. It could be done in stages. It could be begun in Gaza; it could be phased in over a long period of time. It could even be called "autonomy" inside of Israel.

Unfortunately, the benefits associated with the withdrawal will not be sufficient to induce the Israelis to initiate it. The benefits of the two-state solution have been there all the time. But it is always easier to do nothing, and the centrality of Jewish fears can never be underestimated. What is needed to awaken the Israelis to these benefits and to the necessity of withdrawal is a process which makes clear that a continued occupation is untenable. Israeli withdrawal will probably not be achieved until Israel has come to appreciate, not only the benefits of withdrawal, but the high costs associated with failing to withdraw.

Thus, a central part of the non-lethal strategy is to make it increasingly costly for the Israelis to remain, without attempting to exact a toll in Israeli lives. The costs involved come in a variety of forms: economic costs, national security costs, internal discord costs, isolation costs. These overlap and interact; they are just convenient headings for exploring the array of levers at the disposal of a non-lethal strategy and for sharpening an understanding of why, over time, this strategy will succeed.

Economic costs include disruption of the Israeli economy caused by disorderly relations with the territories as markets for Israeli goods, as sources of tax revenue, and as a source of labor for jobs inside Israel. They also include major costs to Israel in terms of tourism, which has dropped precipitously as a result of the Uprising. But economic costs also extend to the failure of Israel to gain the full trade access it had anticipated with the European Economic Community. Costs in these areas have already taken some effect and in some cases will become more severe if Israel refuses to withdraw, although disruption costs will gradually abate as the Israeli economy adjusts to new realities.

When the demand for Israeli withdrawal is coupled with a strong and authentic offer of peace, and with continued protest within the territories against the presence of troops, met by Israeli oppression, the stage will be set for a worldwide campaign of economic pressure. This can take many forms: a boycott of Israeli goods, a boycott on tourism, the withdrawal of trade concessions, and possibly a reduction of foreign aid.

These economic costs will not be severe enough to bring Israel to her knees, which would be impossible in any event. But they will be significant and tangible; they will felt by the average Israeli. Essentially they will get and hold everybody's attention to the continued problem of occupation. And they will hold the possibility of becoming more severe.

Particularly important in this regard will be the United States and the American Jewish community. Only to a marginal degree will American Jews actively participate in a campaign to put economic pressure on Israel. The overwhelming majority of American Jews would regard this as becoming a traitor to their own people. And this feeling will not be overcome by an intellectual awareness that these processes are in Israel's interest and are necessary in order to save her from catastrophe.

However, when the proposal for withdrawal is coupled with a serious peace initiative, many American Jews will come to accept the idea that Israel should indeed withdraw. And when withdrawal is supported by a major segment of Israeli public opinion, this position will gain legitimacy in the American Jewish community, opening new political possibilities within the United States. How far this will go will depend on events. In particular it will depend on the skill and authenticity of the peace initiative and on the nature of the Israeli response. But it is not unthinkable that considerable resistance will develop to continuing to provide Israel with over 3 billion dollars of aid every year. Budgetary pressures within the United States have subjected every other category of spending except aid to Israel to great scrutiny. Such scrutiny will be extended to this special category of spending in the face of broad opposition to Israeli policy, itself a product of broad awareness that the Palestinians and the Arab world are prepared to make peace.

For this to have an impact on Israeli consciousness, actual cuts in foreign aid are not necessary. Indeed, the threat of future cuts may be a more powerful force than the actual impact of any real cuts.[4]

To those who doubt that a change in U.S.-Israeli relations could ever be accomplished within the U.S. government, it is worth noting some of the remarkable things that have already happened. Since the Uprising began in December 1987, thirty senators, without obtaining advance AIPAC approval, signed a letter critical of Prime Minister Shamir's opposition to trading land for peace. And, though it lacks support at the moment, legislation has been introduced to reopen PLO offices in the United States. So has legislation which would declare that the United States Congress supports the idea of an independent Palestinian state in the West Bank and Gaza. Indeed, similar resolutions supporting the Palestinian right of self-determination were passed within the Democratic Party on the state and local levels in 1988. And various highly placed members of the American Jewish community have indicated that they personally could accept an independent Palestinian state on the West Bank and Gaza.[5]

In thinking through the potential within the United States, it must always be remembered that Israel's real strength within the United States is moral strength. The idea that America supports Israel because of the role Israel plays in advancing American national security interests abroad has largely been the concoction of AIPAC's lobbyists on Capitol Hill. Inside the U.S. government, the officials responsible for allocating the security assistance budget look forward to a day when they can shift some of the money that now goes to Israel to various other countries whose needs appear more pressing and whose strategic value to U.S. interests appears greater.

The costs to Israel's national security of continued occupation will take several forms. First, national security resources, both funds and manpower, will be diverted to policing actions that are not germane to Israel's real national security concerns. Second, there will be the risks to Israel's national security posed by prolonged occupation and struggle with the Palestinians. These are serious indeed and have been given insufficient attention by Israeli leaders. The two key elements are the risk of the eventual erosion and breakdown of the Israeli-Egyptian peace treaty and the increasingly radicalized and fundamentalist opposition to Israel fueled by the open conflict with the Palestinians. Third, in the face of a serious peace initiative there would be a loss of unity and morale within the Israeli army.

It would be dangerous indeed if the Egyptian-Israeli peace treaty were to break down. Yet it is completely possible. Egypt remains a politically unstable society, and President Muhammad Hosni Mubarak, having been Sadat's vice-president, is closely linked to the Camp David Accords, which were perceived throughout the Arab world as a sell-out of the Palestinians. Continued Israeli attacks on Palestinian protestors put enormous pressure on Mubarak to distance himself from Israel. Ultimately it was this concern, which the Uprising heightened, which led Mubarak to pressure the United States to launch the Shultz initiative.

This is a very tricky factor. Rationally speaking, concern over the implications of continued struggle with the Palestinians should weigh heavily in Israeli calculations. Yet if the relationship with Egypt appears in doubt, it is likely that the Israelis will become even more reluctant to withdraw from the West Bank and Gaza. For this reason, it would be best for the new State of Palestine to enlist Egyptian and Jordanian cooperation in its peace initiative. Their roles will be most effective as guarantors of the peaceful intent of the Palestinian state and of how Israel can achieve fuller national security by accepting a Palestinian state than by opposing it.

Inside the territories, the Uprising will continue. Indeed, one of the central features of this strategy is that it puts the Uprising of the Palestinian masses within a larger diplomatic and political strategy. Essentially, it provides a long-term raison d'être for the Uprising. This continued challenge to Israeli troops on the ground will be the central driving force behind Israeli withdrawal.

At present, with the PLO strategy tied to the notion of an international conference that somehow will force an independent state upon an unwilling Israel, the role of the Uprising is limited to generating pressures for a conference and for superpower action. As it becomes clear that this, in fact, is not going to happen, the energies of the Uprising will be channeled elsewhere. For many Palestinians it may mean a return to everyday life, more bitter and more cynical. But the failure of the current strategy will lead a significant number of young people, especially those who have been in Israeli prisons, to turn to underground guerrilla activity. This will be dangerous and destructive to the Palestinian cause. One virtue of the alternative strategy outlined here is that a focus on Israeli withdrawal, within the confines of an already declared Palestinian state, will generate constant energy to carry out this task.

Stone-throwing is not incompatible with this strategy. Though violent and dangerous, it is non-lethal: No Israelis have died from having been hit by a stone. Yet stone-throwing is so close to a lethal act, given the size of West Bank stones, that it should be replaced by more clear-cut symbolic acts. But it is likely that it will continue. It has proven itself to be a unique mode of resistance. Stone-throwing allows for the expression of Palestinian rage without endangering the entire community. As an expression of rage it serves as a safety valve reducing pressure to use guns and knives. And because it requires considerable personal courage to hurl a stone at an armed soldier, it has earned Palestinians a measure of respect even from Israeli soldiers. This respect, even so attained, is part of the process whereby Palestinians come to be experienced as full human beings by the Israelis.

Another fundamental aspect of stone-throwing has been ignored: At bottom it is tremendously exciting; at bottom it is fun to throw stones at Israeli soldiers if you are a Palestinian. Even though the risks are high--over two hundred Palestinians have died and thousands have been injured--these confrontations are inherently rewarding. It is like a form of sport; for once the tables are turned on the occupying army. Teenagers and children can defy the army in the most blatant manner. If the stone finds its mark, there is the triumph of having inflicted pain and injury on the adversary. And at this dangerous game, the Israelis for all their fire power can be outsmarted. To the extent that they over-react, they play into the hands of the Palestinians in a larger political battle.

So important has stone-throwing become that young Palestinians tend to react to any suggestion to replace it with nonviolent tactics as a trick to undermine the Uprising. And though they are wrong to impute such motives to the advocates of totally nonviolent tactics, they may well be correct about where the Uprising finds its emotional strength to continue against overwhelming odds.

A line needs to be drawn, and it should be drawn at the distinction between what is lethal and what is not. To some extent this is arbitrary; to some extent it is a matter of intention. That the Palestinians are not trying to kill Israeli soldiers should be made crystal clear. This implies, for instance, declaring a total ban on throwing gasoline bombs.

One goal of the daily confrontations with Israeli soldiers is to shame them. It is to force them to look deeply at themselves and to wonder what it is that they are doing in holding down a civilian population. In the context of a serious peace initiative, which punctures the Israeli psychological defense ("we must do this, or they will go further and further and ultimately drive us into the sea"), this challenge to the self-respect of Israeli soldiers will become increasingly important.

The Israelis have always taken great pride in their armed forces. It is no little thing when the meaning of being a soldier is something to be ashamed of. Yet it is within the power of the Palestinian masses to make the Israelis ashamed of themselves. And they can do this in ways that will be witnessed by the entire world.

One of the lesser-known facts about the Uprising is the extent to which it has employed nonviolent tactics. Especially in the early period, there were peaceful marches, and there were marches by women. Typically, these were dispersed by the use of tear gas, with participants beaten and sometimes jailed. These efforts, unlike throwing stones, involved considerable preparation. They were not covered by the international media, and they involved very high costs for the participants. In short, they were high cost, low benefit options. It is no surprise that they did not become the dominant form of protest.

When Americans ask, "Why don't they do it like the civil rights movement did?," they often are asking for more than they are aware. Let us not underestimate the tremendous courage of the American civil rights movement in passively facing police dogs, cattle prods, and angry mobs. But the civil rights struggle also went on within the context of U.S. law. There was always the federal court system. There was President Eisenhower to nationalize the state militia. There was a John Kennedy and a Bobby Kennedy to call Martin Luther King, Jr. when he was in jail. The Palestinians have no such protections. At this moment, close to two thousand Palestinians are in what is called "administrative detention," imprisoned without charge and without trial. After they have served their six months, they may be given another six months, with no legal protection, and no phone call from an American president.

And the international press, which did play an important role in filming Israeli solders beating civilians, is indeed a fickle resource. After a few months, many of the press corps left Jerusalem and the territories, not because the Uprising had ended but because one day's events looked so much like another. Thus, the Palestinian strategy will have to be constantly creative. It will have to find ways of making sure that the entire world knows what is going on.

One way of ensuring the worldwide coverage so essential to the diplomatic and economic aspects of this strategy is to involve in the struggle individuals whose very presence will compel attention. This might involve leading Israelis, American Jews, worldwide church leaders or artists, writers, and media stars. It might involve U.S. elected officials or former officials; even former presidents should not be ruled out.

How could they be persuaded to come to the West Bank and Gaza, and what would be their role? I believe they would be prepared to come, and in significant numbers, if there were totally nonviolent demonstrations calling for Israeli withdrawal, but also expressing a full commitment to living at peace with Israel.

To date, within the Uprising, it has not been possible to organize such demonstrations. Within the context of the strategy, it would be different. Since living at peace with Israel would be the official policy of the new state, such demonstrations would bring out vast numbers of Palestinians; they could involve virtually the entire population. And foreign visitors could come either as participants or as observers committed at least to the right of the Palestinians to protest peacefully. If the Israeli government were to seal off the West Bank and Gaza to prevent foreign participation and media coverage, then demonstrations could be held inside Israel.

One outcome of this strategy would be to swell the ranks of the Israeli peace movement. Once the Palestinians have declared peace and have offered mutual recognition and negotiations, the struggle inside Israel will be between those who are ideologically and nationalistically committed to holding onto the territories at any cost, and those who see the two-state solution as the great opportunity to ensure that Israel is a secure, democratic, and Jewish state.

The Uprising itself has reawakened the Israeli peace movement. In the first few months, several new groups formed and many who had never participated in demonstrations joined the ranks of the visible opponents of government policy. Increasingly, the Israeli peace movement has gone into the territories to meet with the Palestinians themselves. These contacts between Jews and Palestinians have been powerful events for the participants. The arrival of a few carloads of Israeli Jews who are neither settlers nor soldiers, but ordinary people opposed to the occupation, has often brought Palestinian villagers to tears. In Beita, where the Army leveled Palestinian homes after a young Israeli girl died from the bullet of her escort's gun, villagers and Israelis of the peace movement, who had come to help rebuild houses, embraced and wept in each other's arms.

Interaction between Israelis and Palestinians committed to the two-state solution must be expanded. A central focus of the Israeli peace movement should be to make it possible for Palestinians to enter normal political interaction without fear of reprisal from the Israeli authorities.

Finally, let me say a word about the alternative, about guerrilla attacks as a means of forcing Israeli withdrawal. As stated above, the effort to drive the Israelis out of the West Bank and Gaza through military action is madness that is best quickly forgotten. I have no doubt, however, that this notion will have considerable appeal to some Palestinians, and thus it is important that it be seriously discussed.

In considering this alternative, one must ask: What are the costs, if it fails? What are the chances that it will succeed? Are there better alternatives?

It should be clear to all that if guerrilla action is pursued, and if it fails, it will open the door for mass transfer of the Palestinian population and will mean the end of the new State of Palestine, before it ever comes fully into existence. The argument here is similar to the explanation of why the State of Palestine will never be a serious threat to Israeli national security. It is weak. The Israelis are strong. There is growing sentiment in Israel for some form of expulsion or transfer. The Israelis, when pushed, will act decisively and in surprising ways to protect what they see as their interests.

The term "transfer" should be understood broadly. It need not mean that the entire population of the West Bank and Gaza will be physically transferred to some other state. Such an undertaking might prove impossible. However, there are numerous other kinds of "transfer," all of which have disastrous implications for the Palestinians.

Here are some of the possibilities:

–Gaza becomes the dumping ground. Massive numbers of Palestinians are transferred from the West Bank to Gaza. Once there, they are left to fend for themselves. Gaza is totally sealed off to the outside world. Once evacuated, West Bank villages are totally leveled, just as Palestinian villages were in 1948.

–Within the West Bank, huge new areas are developed as "strategic hamlets." Palestinians are forced to move into these areas "for their own protection" so that the Israelis may isolate the guerrillas and declare areas outside the hamlets "free fire zones." Again, entire villages and cities are emptied. All who remain are defined as "terrorists." Under this definition, Israel uses its air power to decimate West Bank towns and villages.

–Transfer is pursued through a variety of tactics. Suspected guerrillas and political activists are rounded up in very large numbers, say 20,000 to 30,000. A few thousand are physically transferred to Lebanon; the others are put in special camps in the Negev. The families of suspected activists are forced to move to Gaza. Selected villages are punished by total destruction. The West Bank economy is deliberately destroyed by the Israelis; the population is kept just above starvation level; no viable life is permitted. The universities are blown up just to make this clear. At the same time, the Israelis offer "relocation assistance" to any Palestinian wishing to emigrate.

These scenarios just scratch the surface. The Israeli imagination is fertile, and no doubt these and many other alternatives already exist as contingency plans within the advance planning files. What must always be remembered is that the West Bank Palestinians have never felt the full force of Israeli options. The Israelis have been stymied by the political, economic, and moral costs associated with these possibilities. What the Palestinians must never do is to create an environment within which these costs become acceptable to the Israeli public.

Analogies with Israeli withdrawals from both the Sinai and Lebanon are misplaced. In withdrawing from Lebanon the Israelis were not giving up an object of any strong attachment. There were no Jewish settlements in Lebanon; there were no historic claims to Lebanon. More to the point, there never was broad public support for remaining in Lebanon in the first place. The Lebanese war was launched deceitfully; even within the Israeli cabinet, it had been presented as a limited incursion with a short-term military purpose. Further, it should be noted that Israel never had any real national security fears associated with Lebanon; it did not fear that withdrawal would lead to the creation of a state dedicated to its destruction. Finally, it should be remembered that some Israeli troops are still in Lebanon, Israeli planes still bomb targets in Lebanon, and Israeli troops periodically surge forth into areas from which they previously withdrew.

The situation in the West Bank and Gaza is totally different. If the Israelis were militarily forced out of the West Bank and Gaza, they would be leaving behind a significant military enemy, victorious and filled with self-confidence. The implications of this would be absolutely unacceptable to virtually all Israelis. Thus, they would be prepared to pay a very high price to prevent this from occurring.

I am not saying that it is logically impossible that at some level of Israeli deaths the Israelis would say, "Okay, it is not worth it, let's withdraw." What I am saying is that this hypothetical level of Israeli deaths is not a matter of a few hundred, or even a few thousand. But let us assume that some such level exists. Suppose it is 10,000, that is, one out of every 350 Israeli Jews. Before the Palestinians could inflict 10,000 deaths on the Israeli armed forces, the Israelis could inflict a million deaths on the Palestinians. Or more to the point, they could initiate any one of a dozen scenarios to prevent the Israeli death toll from ever approaching such numbers. And as horrible as 10,000 deaths might be, it is far, far from the number Israel is capable of sustaining, if it feels it has no other choice. It will feel this if it believes it is facing an option of die now or die later. A massive guerrilla movement in the West Bank and Gaza will trigger the worst fears in the Israeli psyche; there will be no way of convincing Israelis that peace is possible if they withdraw under those circumstances. Needless to say, these considerations will only be reinforced if the scenario involves conflict with one or more of the Arab states.

These issues are so critical to the Palestinian cause, and to the survival of the new State of Palestine, that ultimately Yasser Arafat may be forced to do something that he has always refrained from doing. If the new state comes into being, he will have to be prepared to use the full force of the state to prevent individuals and independent guerrilla groups, operating from the West Bank and Gaza, from taking matters into their own hands. In this, his situation will be similar to that of Ben Gurion, who, once the State of Israel came into existence, used the Israeli army against Begin's guerrilla organization, the Irgun. Once it was clear that the authority of the state had to be respected, Begin fell in line. Whether or not Arafat will actually have to use force to gain respect for the authority of the state is not clear; what is clear is that he must be prepared to do so.

Building the Inner Sinews of Statehood

The Israeli troops continue to occupy the West Bank and Gaza. This poses two problems for the Palestinians, and they are intimately related. The first problem is how the Israelis can be made to leave. The second is how, while they are there, the Palestinian state can come more fully into being. The previous section considered the various means of inducing Israeli withdrawal; this section considers the processes whereby the Palestinian state will emerge.

I have used terms such as "emerge" and "come more fully into being" in order to emphasize that the creation of a state may be a process, rather than a single event. A state may slowly come to exist and may slowly go out of existence. It is one thing to declare the existence of the state; it is something else to give it reality.

It may be thought that so long as the Israeli troops occupy the West Bank and Gaza, Palestinian statehood is mere verbiage. Yet what is the logic of this position? What exactly is it about the presence of Israeli troops that is incompatible with the existence of a Palestinian state? Consider, for instance, their numbers. Suppose that there are ten thousand Israeli troops in the West Bank; surely this fact in itself is not incompatible with the existence of the Palestinian state. The troops could be there as guests or as tourists. In itself, the physical presence of Israeli troops means nothing; they are simply foreigners who have a certain profession.

If the Israeli troops are incompatible with Palestinian statehood, the problem is not their mere presence in the West Bank but their role. But what exactly do they do that makes Palestinian statehood unreal? They rule. But what exactly is it to rule? Surely, it is more than the fact that they give orders; it must be that the people obey their orders. But if this is true, then if the people stop obeying, the Israelis stop ruling. And if they stop ruling, then perhaps a Palestinian state can exist while they are there.

This puts the matter of civil disobedience in a totally different light. The situation is quite unlike that of the U.S. civil rights movement where civil disobedience was a tactic, a way of protesting an unjust law or calling attention to a righteous cause. In the Uprising, civil disobedience may have this function too, but that is not what it is really about. For the Uprising is a struggle over who rules, and disobedience is not merely a way of protesting a specific injustice or even of calling attention to the general injustice of Israeli rule. Civil disobedience, when carried out by the entire population, *constitutes* the cessation of Israeli rule. In and of itself every act of civil disobedience is a victory for the Palestinians.

This goes to the heart of what the Uprising is about. Not only is it a matter of not obeying, it is a matter of confronting the Israelis with the fact that they are not obeyed. It must always be remembered that the kind of obedience that a government commands differs from the kind commanded by a robber. A government is obeyed even when it is not directly present, even when it does not point a gun at you, even when it does not threaten at all. That is what makes it a government, and this is true even of unpopular and morally illegitimate governments.

So this matter of obedience proves to be quite subtle. The Palestinian people can change the status of the Israeli army simply by obeying the Israelis only at gun point. And this, in fact, is exactly what the Uprising has started. It is in this sense that the Israelis have already lost effective control of the territories.

But this is only part of the story. For while there is no longer a functioning Israeli government in the territories, the presence of Israeli soldiers can block the emergence of any alternative government. But again, the army does not do this through its mere presence, but either by eliminating any group purporting to be the alternative rule-giver, i.e., the government, or by preventing the people from obeying the new rule-giver.

These points may all seem remote and philosophical. Actually they are implicitly understood both by the Israelis and by the Palestinian population. And it is because they both understand this that the Uprising has taken the form that it has. A struggle over who is obeyed, over who rules in the territories, is exactly what has been going on. And these confrontations are just as weighty when they are over purely symbolic issues as they are when they concern tangible and overt disagreements.

Consider some of the scenes we have all witnessed. The Israelis impose a curfew on Gaza; they assert that after 6:00 p.m. anyone found on the street will be shot. The soldiers are there to enforce the command. Everyone obeys. But then the next day, the Underground announces a curfew of its own. They say that no stores will open until 5:00 p.m. There are no Palestinian soldiers, but out of allegiance, community pressure, and some fear, the people obey this curfew too. The Israeli soldiers take out their crow bars. They force open the shops. And while they stand there, the shops remain open. But as soon as they move to the next block, the shopkeepers close them down again. What is going on? Clearly there is a struggle over who gives the orders on the West Bank, or to put it more accurately, a struggle over whose orders are obeyed.

Travel through Gaza and look up. You will see dozens of small Palestinian flags hanging from electrical wires. How did they get there? Young children tied rocks to flags with short strings. They threw them at the wires, the rocks spun around the wires, and the flags were made secure. It takes a minute to get one up; it takes an hour to get one down. The soldiers were defeated. Every flag announces that the Israelis do not rule.

The Underground command is comprised mainly of the PLO. Somehow it manages to meet, to discuss issues, to resolve differences, to draft orders, and to distribute leaflets announcing those orders throughout the territories. The Israelis have not been able to figure out who they are and how to stop them. Essentially, the Underground command is functioning as an inchoate government. Once the State of Palestine is declared, the command leaders will be government officials.

The struggle with the Israelis over who rules the territories involves more than confronting them with the fact that they no longer rule and that the people are marching to a different drummer. Governments are not mere roosters crowing their existence. They have jobs to perform, functions that people want and need governments for. Identify those functions, and you have identified the process of bringing the Palestinian state into being. It is largely a matter of finding a way for the new state to carry out its governmental functions, whether the Israelis like it or not. If this can be done, the state will exist.

That the Israeli troops remain of itself proves something. It proves that the government is weak, that it is not the complete master of its house. But it proves nothing more than this. And every government is weak; no government is the full master of its house. Like it or not, the United States government cannot prevent illegal immigrants from entering the country; it cannot force drug pushers off the streets; it cannot get muggers out of Central Park. And this is to say nothing of its inability to house the poor, end unemployment, or provide adequate care for the elderly. It is the nature of modern governments that they have problems they cannot solve.

The continued presence of the Israeli troops can be transformed into a social problem. The State of Palestine wants them to go home; it is working on the problem; it is looking for a Pied Piper to lead them away, but it hasn't yet found the solution. It is not within the power of the Palestinian population of the territories to expel the Israelis but it is within their power to reduce them to size, to transform them from a ruling army to something akin to illegal aliens.

The Israelis, of course, are fighting back. The Palestinians stop paying taxes. The Israelis require proof of paid taxes in order to have a driver's license. The Underground considers calling on everyone to burn their driver's licenses; but it hesitates. Does it dare? What if it orders everyone to do it and most people do not? The costs of not being obeyed are high.

The Palestinians try to organize. The Israelis counter by arresting people and imprisoning them without any charges or trial; soldiers break into homes and destroy property. Israeli lawlessness demonstrates one thing: the Palestinians do not have any police power. They have no sheriff, no cop on the beat. In short, no government exists: this is the implicit message of Israeli attacks. But the provisional government can respond–not by directly confronting the troops, but by making the costs of Israeli lawlessness too high. And if it succeeds in doing this, it succeeds in bringing safety to the villages. The cop on the beat is only a means to an end; if the government can achieve the same end indirectly, it has been successful. Thus, protecting its people from abuse is an end to be pursued for a variety of reasons: for the sake of the people, for the sake of promoting Israeli withdrawal, and for demonstrating that the provisional government does take on and carry out the functions of government.

Against what standard does one measure the functioning of the Palestinian state? What is the appropriate benchmark? This raises a very interesting issue. How adequately the Palestinian state, under Israeli occupation, will be able to carry out its governing functions depends on what one takes those functions to be. If one is a libertarian the answer will be different than if one is a believer in a planned economy or a totalitarian system. Against the benchmark of a minimal state, it is possible for the Palestinian state to do quite well. What it must accomplish are three things:

1. the erosion of Israeli rule,

2. the introduction of a functioning criminal justice system, and

3. the establishment of some procedures for adjudicating civil disputes.

These are the basics. There are many other things governments sometimes do, e.g., licensing drivers or firearms, owning factories, or building schools. But these are not essential government functions. They can either be dispensed with entirely or carried out by non-governmental organizations. Indeed, current thinking on the role of government in the Third World is that it has attempted to do too much. A major theme articulated by many development experts is "privatization," the return to the private or voluntary sector of functions that the state had previously assumed. Of necessity, the Palestinian government will start off not making some of the mistakes that have plagued other Third World states.

To carry out its essential functions, any state needs some ability to raise and spend funds, an ability to appoint officials, and some means of punishment and adjudication. If the Palestinian state under occupation can do this much, it will have established its existence. If in addition, it can carry out more ambitious tasks, it will triumph decisively.

When we speak of the state carrying out certain functions, there is a tendency to imagine that these must be undertaken by the central government. Clearly this is not so. In the United States, many of the most important governmental functions are the responsibility of local governments. For instance, with respect to education, the federal government plays a limited role; in the main, policy and financing occur on the state and local levels.

The fact that some functions not only can be carried out locally but are best decentralized makes the task of the Palestinian state considerably easier. For instance, there is no need for a national police force, nor for a national system of courts. Just as in the United States, these functions can be handled locally, so long as they operate outside the administrative mechanisms established by the Israelis. Indeed, in some instances it may even be possible to retain those mechanisms but to have their real functioning determined by the new state and not by the military administration.

In the struggle to resist the reality of the Palestinian state, it is to be expected that the Israeli government will do what it can to prevent the functioning of a Palestinian government on any level, local or national. So it is unlikely that the Israelis will allow the reinstitution of local elections if it is clear that the elected mayors would affirm their loyalty to the new state. Similarly, the Israelis will not allow local police, local courts, and local taxes. They will prevent these functions from being carried out by arresting and imprisoning anyone who attempts them.

This then sets the terms for the Uprising: how can it carry out these functions on the local level in the face of Israeli opposition? There are several threads to the answer. First one can learn a great deal from anarchists. Anarchism has a bad name because it is associated with lawlessness. But as a serious social philosophy, anarchism maintains that the state is unnecessary. It argues that human beings, both as individuals and as communities, can provide for themselves and for each other without depending upon governmental structures. In the Reagan Administration, this strain of thought emerged under the term "voluntarism"—reliance on voluntary contributions instead of on taxes and on fraternal and charitable organizations rather than on government.

One need not accept the entire anarchist framework to recognize its great relevance for the Palestinian state. The magnitude of the problems faced by the government, for instance, in dealing with criminality depends on two factors: the extent of criminality and the extent to which there are adequate non-governmental responses to it. Thus, ordinary people throughout the territories can help make the new government work by making things easier for it.

There is at least anecdotal evidence that this is exactly what has been happening during the Uprising, though it has occurred without the benefit of a theoretical framework explaining why it needs to occur. For instance, under Israeli administration, large numbers of Palestinians worked for the Israelis as policemen. One of the first acts of the Underground was to call for the resignation of these Palestinian police. And they did resign in large numbers. It was predicted that one consequence would be a vast upsurge in crime. In fact, it appears that this has not happened.

If there is little crime, or if the public participates in the apprehension of criminals, then with a thin layer of police and a minimal court system localities can successfully run a criminal justice system. And they can do this largely underground. Just as there are today underground printers and underground couriers, so too there can be an occasional underground judge or marshall. So quickly we forget how little actual government is needed. In U.S. history, it was not so long ago that many towns were serviced by circuit judges and marshalls. When you have well-established communities in which everyone is known to everyone else, and when the populace is highly motivated to solve problems collectively, there is no question that order can be maintained with a thin layer of officialdom. With no large bureaucracy, there is no need for significant taxes. A simple headtax on each Palestinian family, perhaps based on a rough categorization of income, is all that is needed both to finance these local services and symbolically to reaffirm the existence of the state.

Every society has to decide which functions will be entrusted to government and which functions will be carried out by religious institutions. Thus the establishment of regulations and processes dealing with birth, education, marriage, divorce, death, and inheritance fall differentially within the purview of

both religious and secular authorities. Clearly conditions of occupation that limit the role of the state open the way for an expanded role for religious authorities. This can serve to increase
the independence from Israeli-controlled institutions. On the
other hand, it has implications of far-reaching significance and,
depending on the politics of the religious factions, could ultimately be highly counterproductive to the establishment of
peace and the viability of the Palestinian state. Palestinians will
have to think carefully about the appropriate role of religious institutions.

At present, both in Gaza and in the West Bank, many social
services ranging from education to medical care are provided by
foreign donors. Some of these come from the United Nations organizations, some from governmental aid programs (e.g., from
the United States and from the Scandinavian countries), and
some from private and church groups (e.g., Save the Children,
Catholic Relief Services). To the extent that these non-Israeli
avenues can be expanded, dependence on Israeli administration
is lessened. The new government should make a concerted effort
to step up these forms of assistance. It is quite possible that the
Israelis will move to close them down, but if they do, they will
be incurring the anger and opposition of well-placed and well-
respected groups throughout the world.

In dealing with the Uprising, the Israeli strategy appears to be
to increase pressure on the population, in the hope that this will
generate resentment against political activists and ultimately
break the resistance. Thus one Israeli policy is to cut back on social services provided by the military administration. *The
Washington Post* reported:

> The military administration has stopped making welfare and
> hospital payments to needy families and cut off funds for local
> authorities, health services, sewage and drinking water systems,
> road building and electricity grids while it searches for funds, ac-
> cording to the [Israeli] official. . . .[6]

In its press relations, the Israelis have presented these cutbacks
as necessitated by financial conditions created by the Palestinian
refusal to pay taxes. Obviously, however, the financial factors
are secondary.

It is very unlikely that these pressure tactics will bring the desired result. Indeed, they may be welcomed by the leadership of the Uprising. One of their goals has been to create economic self-reliance, to sever ties with and dependency on the Israelis. While in the short run the disruption of social services will occasion considerable hardship, this will likely abate as time goes on, and as Palestinians find alternative ways of meeting their social needs. In deliberately cutting off social services the Israelis are abandoning one of the functions of the Israeli governmental structure; in short, they are unwittingly helping to phase themselves out of existence.

The issue of self-reliance does raise one major issue for both the Uprising and the Palestinian state: its links to the Israeli economy. Before the Uprising, roughly one-third of the Palestinian labor force worked in Israel. Everyday this massive manpower pool would enter Israeli territory, and every evening it would return home to the West Bank and Gaza.

Here, too, there has been a strange coming together of the tactics of the Uprising and of the Israeli efforts to put down the insurrection. At different points the Uprising has called on people not to work in Israel; at the same time the Israelis have tried to break the Uprising by refusing identity cards, necessary in order to enter Israel, to Palestinians who have not paid their taxes. In effect the two sides have placed different bets on the Palestinian psyche.

But should the fledgling Palestinian state deliberately cut all ties with the Israeli economy? I would advise against it for several reasons. First, this will not be necessary to firm up the sense of Palestinian identity. Second, the willingness of Palestinians who come to regard themselves as citizens of the State of Palestine to work in Israel reinforces the belief that permanent peaceful relations between the two states are possible. Third, with the new pride that will come from the end to statelessness, the daily presence of these Palestinians inside Israel could have a valuable impact on Israeli attitudes. And finally, the new state will need resources; the earnings from employment in Israel, even if they are much less than what Israelis earn, are substantial on an aggregate basis.

This is not to say that Palestinians should work in Israel under all circumstances. For instance, if the Israelis continue to demand proof of payment of taxes before they will admit daily workers, it might be best to forego admission. This, of course, will mean some serious decline in the Palestinian standard of living. And it is possible that the Israelis will find ways of blocking outside assistance. Thus, the new state will be forced to struggle forward under economic burdens.

While this will be a significant hardship, it will not be unbearable. The standard of living within the West Bank is well above that achieved by many Third World nations; a highly motivated people, willing to share the burdens, will be able to bear up under these pressures. In Gaza the conditions are more severe, and there is greater dependency on income derived from employment within Israel. One cannot be cavalier about the hardships that may be ahead. Yet the fact remains that economic pressure, short of inducing deliberate starvation, has little coercive power over a politically aroused population. Indeed, common hardship accepted in a common cause tends to deepen rather than undermine commitment.

Development

It is one thing to speak of bringing the Palestinian state into being; it is another to ask if that state will be able to undertake the major tasks at hand. For the West Bank, and even more so for Gaza, the central task is that which occupies all Third World nations. It is the task of development.

The issue of development is not peripheral to the issue of peace. On one level it arises as the question of the so-called "economic viability" of a Palestinian mini-state. Unless such a state can be shown to be economically viable, it is claimed, it is unreasonable to view the two-state option as the solution to the conflict. I have never been impressed by this line of argument, but it is worth discussing. More to the point, however, is the fact that a stable peace will take hold in the Middle East only, if the parties are able, in the deepest sense, to put the conflict behind them.

The Palestinians have for generations been engaged in the project of resisting, of hanging on, of forming a national identity, and of winning their political liberation. To put the conflict into the past, they will require some other central project into which their passion and hopes can naturally flow. There is really only one candidate project, and in some ways, it is an even more compelling project than securing negative freedom from the rule of others. It is the positive project of doing something with that freedom, taking their new state and using it to create a society within which the Palestinian people can flourish. And hopefully, when the conflict is behind them, the Israelis will be able to return to their version of that project, too.

An interesting dialectic is at work here. To the extent that the development project can begin even while Israeli occupation persists, this will not only deepen the reality of the existence of the new state, but it will make ever more clear to all concerned that the conflict is coming to a close. It will make clear that not only have the Palestinians been able to create their state without Israeli permission, but they are able to create the psychological and socioeconomic conditions of a stable peace without Israeli cooperation. This reality–that the Palestinians are in fact turning toward something more fundamental than fighting Israel, toward the creation of a vibrant society–will itself play an important role in increasing the pressures for Israeli withdrawal.

But surely it seems impossible for this Palestinian state, initiated through an act of will in solidarity with a popular uprising, to undertake the enormous tasks of development while fighting for its very existence under Israeli military occupation. Is it not obvious that the major functions of government in the development process could not possibly be carried out under these conditions? How could the Palestinian state build roads or power plants, or undertake investments in agriculture or new industries? How could it initiate a development plan? In short, how could it mobilize and concentrate the energies of the society toward those things that vitally need doing?

The answer here parallels what we have said about the very existence of the state. How one assesses what is possible depends on how one thinks about what is necessary. Certainly

some crucial tasks will simply have to be delayed until some accommodation with the Israelis is reached. Conceivably, it will be
possible to initiate major development projects such as the
building of needed infrastructure even prior to complete Israeli
withdrawal. This is one area in which the United States, if it were
so disposed, could play a useful role.

But if Israeli opposition remains strong, is there any way in
which the Palestinian people could launch their development efforts regardless, with Israeli troops in their midst?

It all depends on what one means by development and how
one goes about achieving it. To the extent that development
means vast construction, the answer is clearly no. Anything that
the Palestinians could build, the Israelis could blow up. And indeed, no small amount of Palestinian rage at the over two
decades of Israeli rule comes from a reaction to Israeli efforts to
prevent energetic Palestinians from bettering their own lot, from
expanding their homes, and from building up local industries.

The question of development has two aspects, neither of
which has ever received a fully satisfactory answer from experts.
The first is simply the question of ends, goals, and objectives.
Just what is it that the development process is attempting to
bring about? What is a developed society? The second is the
question of means, processes, and policies. Just how does one go
about promoting development? In particular, what is the role of
government in the development process? Clearly, one can never
feel comfortable with any answer to the second set of questions
until one has resolved the first. If you do not know what you
should be aiming at, how can you know you have the right way
of bringing it about? But even insofar as there have been relatively settled answers to the first set of questions, the thinking about
how to bring about development has undergone serious and
continuous revision.

For instance, if the goal of development is defined as equitable
growth—higher average incomes coupled with a more even distribution of income—there has been a major shift in thinking
about how this is to be achieved. An early model, which many
nations followed, was that government should nationalize in-
dustry, develop detailed investment plans for controlling the al-

location of resources within the economy, and institute major subsidies on basic commodities. Egypt stands out as an example of this development path. And for a decade now, with only limited success, Egypt has been struggling to free itself of this approach. An alternative model deemphasizes the role of government and notes that the beneficiaries of subsidy programs in the Third World have typically been members of the middle class rather than the poor.

We do not have to settle these issues here. There is sufficient variety with respect to both the goals and means of development to allow us to ask a more pointed question: What kind of development might be feasible under conditions of Israeli occupation?

Several characteristics can be noted:

1. On the strictly economic level, the State of Palestine will not prosper on the basis of vast natural resources. It will prosper on the basis of what it already has: human resources. Economists talk about investing in human capital. The term is a bit grotesque, but it captures the fact that the human being is ultimately the most important productive resource, and that investments in human development are lifelong investments whose benefits spread not only to the next generation, but laterally as well. The Palestinians are already the most educated of the Arab peoples. Their college graduates are in key professional positions throughout the Arab world. This human capital is their major economic resource. The Israelis cannot destroy it, and it can be built upon even under conditions of occupation.

2. A society born out of social struggle will clearly have a strong orientation toward equity. In the industrialized world, the effect of both world wars was to break down barriers of privilege and to empower the poor. Certainly for the Palestinians, whose struggle has been waged in large part by the poorer groups in society and by people living in refugee encampments, it will be totally unacceptable for life after liberation to mean gross social inequities and limited horizons for the average person.

This factor, which can be viewed as either a demand or an opportunity, can be addressed now. Indeed, development experience has shown that equitable development is not achieved by economic growth first and redistribution later. Rather it is achieved by empowering the poor with the resources of high productivity and hence with higher earnings at the earliest stages of the growth process.

In all instances, a central productive resource is education. Thus, if the Palestinian economy is going to rest to a considerable extent on human capital, equity there will rest on the equitable distribution of that capital. This means an educational revolution for the poorer segments of Palestinian society, ensuring that all Palestinians are relatively equally empowered educationally. Certainly energies might focus on this goal even under occupation.

3. The society that the Palestinians are struggling for remains to be defined by them. But this process of definition by the people means that economic and political decision-making will have to involve the broad participation of the masses. Conditions of occupation and minimal state power are in some ways ideally suited for the building of democratic and egalitarian traditions. When there is no powerful state, there is, to use Marxist language, no instrumentality of class coercion. Thus the period in which the state is coming into being, the period under Israeli occupation, is a time of a great opportunity and ultimately the formative period within which the character of the future Palestinian society will be determined. It is the time during which democratic and participatory traditions are to be developed.

4. Closely related to the issue of equity is the question of women. In the last decade this has come to be known as the issue of "women in development." The term covers not merely the question of whether or not women and girls benefit from the development process, but whether or not it utilizes their full potentials. These issues are obviously more than merely economic or political matters. They go to the heart of the kind of society and culture that any people seeks to bring about. Revolutionary struggles, such as the current uprising, tend to promote the liberation of women. When it comes to an all-out struggle,

the contributions of women, as of the poor, are too important to be restricted by narrow tradition. But obviously the issue is complex. Traditionalist and fundamentalist forces sometimes find their place within political struggles, and women may find their lives regulated as never before. For Palestinian women and men, especially in the light of the growing role of Islamic fundamentalism in the political struggle, these questions will increasingly come to the fore.

Palestinian women already play an important part in the Uprising, but they are not out front. There are no women members of the PLO executive committee, and one doubts if there are women in the underground leadership. If Palestinian women are to have a full place in the future Palestinian society, they will have to wage a struggle within the struggle.

To some all of this may seem premature. What could be more a matter of getting the cart before the horse than to begin to engage development issues intellectually, socially, and practically prior to securing full independence. My answer is just the reverse. This is the time to begin. Later is too late. Like it or not, this is the formative period; and in any event the process has already begun.

The Symbols of Statehood

Certain universal symbolic features are shared by all modern governments. All countries have flags, national anthems, national currencies, stamps, and passports. These are things we take for granted, but they are absent when one is stateless, when one lives in an "occupied territory." As soon as the new State of Palestine is declared, it will be possible to leap forward in these areas. Each of these features of statehood presents special problems and calls for a unique approach. But collectively they will contribute a good deal to the sense that the state does in fact exist; that Palestine is a country.

Flags

The Palestinians already have a flag: red, white, green, and black. And it is already a symbol of resistance. Its display is illegal, and Israeli soldiers go to great lengths to remove Palestinian flags whenever they see them. And Palestinian teenagers go to great lengths to find ways of displaying them that will be resistant to Israeli counter-efforts. So far, it seems that the teenagers are winning.

But the Palestinian flag is not yet a state flag. This requires only that there be a state and that it so designate the existing flag. Once done, the flags will fly in every country that recognizes the new state. It can fly in the halls of international organizations. And it can fly at the Olympics.

The Olympics, in fact, are a perfect illustration of the way a state can give the Palestinian people a new beginning. Of all the acts of terrorism connected with the Israeli-Palestinian struggle, none was more dramatic and damaging to the Palestinian cause than the taking hostage of the Israeli athletes at the 1972 Munich Olympics. With terrorism and lethal attacks on Israelis behind them, the new Palestinian state should seek admission to the next Olympic games. Hopefully, the Israelis would not boycott the games, and while they would, no doubt, refuse to compete against Palestinian athletes, Palestinian willingness to participate would be a dramatic statement of the distance that the Palestinian struggle had come. And if Israeli athletes did compete against Palestinian athletes, this would open the way to Israeli-Palestinian sports competition on a regular basis. Who knows, dreamers might even talk of someday having confederated teams.

National Currencies

It is one of the unique prerogatives of states to issue money. And money being money, it always gets taken seriously. Indeed, as we all know, money overcomes all sorts of obstacles.

To be taken seriously, the Palestinian currency has to be a hard currency. That is, it has to be convertible into a currency that is respected worldwide. Let it be convertible on a one-to-one basis with the dollar. One Palestinian dollar should be equal in value to one U.S. dollar. To accomplish this, all that is necessary is a trusted guarantor who will stand willing to exchange American dollars for Palestinian dollars. Once this is done, no one will sneeze at the Palestinian dollar. Indeed, it is highly probable that the average Israeli, be he soldier or settler, Likud or Labor, will not burn Palestinian dollars when they are worth one U.S. dollar each.

The Arab states can take on the role as guarantor of the Palestinian currency, through full agreement between the new Palestinian government and the Arab states. Limits would have to be set on the amount of Palestinian currency to be issued. The Arab states could not be expected to take on an open-ended commitment. But let us suppose that they agreed to back one billion Palestinian dollars. Think of what that would mean.

One of the remarkable things about money is that it gains its value simply by virtue of being trusted. If the Arab states were to announce that they were prepared to exchange Palestinian dollars for U.S. dollars, the new government could simply print up one billion Palestinian dollars and start spending them. If all were redeemed, of course, it would have cost the Arab states one billion dollars to do this. But in fact, for the most part the new Palestinian dollars would simply enter circulation and stay in circulation. And any that were redeemed by Arab governments could again be recirculated, so long as their redemption was trusted. In this way, not only could the new currency be introduced, but the new state could be given a billion-dollar assist.

This may sound magical. In fact it is the same as what occurs when a very large bank gives someone a very large loan by issuing him or her a checkbook (a sheaf of paper with the bank's name on it) and agreeing that he can "issue" checks up to the amount of the loan, with the bank standing behind him. If the checks never return to the bank, the bank never even lays out any cash.

Once a convertible Palestinian currency is in circulation, it will have an exchange rate with every currency that exchanges with the U.S. dollar. It will be listed in the bank windows of every country where it circulates. And because the Israeli sheckel is convertible into U.S. dollars, at a fluctuating rate, there will be sheckel/Palestinian dollar conversions. Indeed, these will occur all the time if the currency can be smuggled into the territories. And once present, it will make no difference if the Israeli government declares Palestinian currency illegal. No government has ever been able to stamp out the black market, and there is no reason to think that individual Israelis will be above trading in Palestinian dollars. The extent of Israeli governmental efforts and penalties, and the extent of Israeli sentiment against use of the Palestinian dollar, will simply be reflected in the discount rate.

Thus, to compensate for the risks of taking Palestinian dollars, it might be necessary to discount them to eighty-five American cents to each Palestinian dollar. The great triumph of this is that the State of Israel and the State of Palestine will be recognizing each other in every currency exchange. There is no telling how far this might go. It is not beyond possibility that the Israeli government might just give up and not even try to suppress the Palestinian currency.

These ideas may be extended in a variety of ways. One could imagine that the Arab countries would allow traveler's checks to be issued in Palestinian dollars. Thus, any Arab citizen could go to an Arab bank and purchase for the equivalent of say, 100 American dollars, 100 dollars worth of Palestinian traveler's checks. Certainly within the Arab world these could be honored by all businesses, and this could be extended to European countries as well. The traveler's checks, denominated in Palestinian dollars, would be fully backed by the issuing banks, and since they would be equivalent in value to U.S. dollars, they would be very easy to introduce. In ways of this sort, the entire world would soon be accepting the symbols of Palestinian statehood. This is called "creating facts."

Within the territories, it might be best to introduce a small coin rather than paper money. Such is the beauty of coins, and their ancient mysterious nature, that the new coins of the State of Palestine would be extremely exciting. They too would be convertible into U.S. dollars, but because it might prove difficult to get them out of the country, they should have some intrinsic worth. Thus, a single coin, equal to, say, ten dollars might be issued, with enough gold content to give it an intrinsic value of, say, five dollars. Stamped "State of Palestine" and decorated with the dove of peace or the olive branch, these would be powerful symbols. Once again, every time they were used to make a purchase or pay a debt, Palestinian statehood would be affirmed and national identity reinforced.

Postage Stamps

Along with money, states have a monopoly on issuing postage stamps. All states belong to an international postal agreement whereby they agree to deliver letters within their countries regardless of where they come from, so long as they carry a stamp issued by the country of origin.

While the Israeli military continues to occupy the West Bank and Gaza, it will not be possible for the State of Palestine to issue stamps from its home territories. But it could work out cooperative agreements with many other nations of the world, whereby a nation in cooperation with the State of Palestine would issue a Palestinian stamp. It would be jointly marked by the two states, and in some instances revenues from its sale could even be given to the new state.

These stamps would not only be used inside the cooperating states, but being jointly issued, they would be valid in all international mailings. Thus, beautiful new stamps, perhaps as many as one hundred of them, originating from one hundred different nations, would appear. They would be used not only by Palestinians and Arabs, but by anyone who supports the two-state solution. Thus the very act of mailing a letter would become a way of showing support for the new state.

Passports

Another prerogative of states is to issue passports. Passports are more than symbols. They are internationally respected documents that individuals use in exercising their right to enter and leave foreign countries. It is part of what it is to be stateless that many Palestinians can obtain no passport, and none can obtain a Palestinian passport.

The new state should promptly issue its own passports. These, of course, could not be issued to Palestinians living under Israeli military occupation, but they could be issued to all other Palestinians. Those in Lebanon, and those who are merely resident aliens in other states, would be the first in need. But the new state could also announce that it will allow dual citizenship, and thus it could call upon all Palestinians to apply for Palestinian passports. Because these would be accepted by most of the nations of the world, all Palestinians, regardless of their other citizenship, should be urged to travel on Palestinian passports. And someday, they will use them to travel to the new State of Palestine.

Expanded Links to Jewish Groups

In recent years, successive meetings of the Palestine National Council (PNC) have passed resolutions articulating a policy of expanded contact with Israelis. Specifically the PNC resolutions adopted in April 1987 called for:

> Developing the relations with the Israeli democratic forces which support the Palestinian people's struggle against occupation and Israeli expansion and which support our people's inalienable national rights including its right to return, to self-determination and to establish its independent state. ... [7]

In fact, actual PLO policy has been broader than this wording suggests. Arafat himself has taken a leadership role in personally meeting with Jews who might not subscribe to all the principles articulated above. The reason he has given priority to such meetings is that he recognizes that ultimately a political solution is necessary, and that it will not be brought about by some towering Israeli political leader, but by a shift in Israeli public opinion.[8]

The Israeli government moved to counter this tendency by passing legislation making it illegal for any Israeli citizen to meet with PLO representatives without formal government permission. In June 1988, four Israelis–Reuvin Kaminer, Elizer Feiler, Latif Dori, and Yael Lotan, all members of the peace movement– were found guilty of meeting with PLO representatives in

Rumania in 1986. These were not secret meetings; they were announced with considerable publicity as a way of opening dialogue with the PLO.

In the United States, no law prevents citizens from meeting with the PLO. Rather, law and policy prevent government officials from negotiating with the PLO. With respect to American citizens, in particular mainstream leaders of the American Jewish community, it is their own unwillingness to meet with PLO representatives that has prevented such meetings from occurring.

While these policies and personal attitudes have foolishly failed to take advantage of opportunities to contribute to the fuller evolution and moderation of the PLO that has occurred over the years, they are not particularly surprising. So long as the PLO refused explicitly to accept Israel's right to exist and was prepared to carry out terrorist attacks within Israel, it would be very difficult to find a politician, Israeli or American, or a Jewish-American leader, who would meet with the PLO simply on the basis that it might be helpful to the cause of peace. Indeed, the U.S. Jewish community has sought to limit contact with the PLO not just for American Jews, but for all Americans. Great and effective pressure was placed on the executive branch, which resulted in the closure of the PLO information office in Washington. Subsequently, legislation was passed requiring the closure not only of the Washington office, but of the PLO Observer Mission at the United Nations as well.

Although Secretary of State Shultz condemned this legislation as among "the dumber acts of Congress," it has not been repealed and was widely supported by Jewish-American leaders. They did not even argue about the legislation's impact on the prospects for peace. The internal debate focused on the civil liberties aspects of using the government to close the offices of an organization reviled by most American Jews.

The creation of the Palestinian state, coupled with the measures discussed above (unilateral declaration of peace, offer to exchange ambassadors, offer to negotiate a final peace treaty, legislation outlawing terrorism, and a policy forbidding lethal attacks on Israeli soldiers), will collectively have a revolutionary impact on Jewish attitudes in the United States and Israel. It is not well-known, but a substantial part of the American Jewish community has always been willing to accept a Palestinian state if it could be sure that such a state would be no threat to Israel.

As one part of the peace initiative, the new state should launch a major drive to open lines of contact with Jews around the world. The Israeli government will probably make this illegal for Israeli citizens. Many Israelis will respond in any event. In the United States, where it is still possible for citizens to decide whom they will talk to, the new government should seek meetings with every significant Jewish organization in the country. And it should send representatives to every synagogue or Jewish community center that will invite them. What is needed is a new style of people-to-people diplomacy. Palestinian Americans, having become dual citizens of the United States and Palestine, would be perfect ambassadors to the American Jewish community.

So long as the Israeli government opposes contact with the new government of Palestine, the American Jewish community, as a collective body, will not challenge that edict. For too long, many Jewish-American leaders have defined their role and responsibilities as knee-jerk support for any Israeli government policy.

On the other hand, while it is unlikely that the leaders of AIPAC and the Conference of Presidents of Major Jewish Organizations will meet with the new President of the State of Palestine, it is likely that many of the more liberal Jewish organizations and their leaders will. Thus, the American Jewish Committee, the American Jewish Congress, and the Union of American Hebrew Congregations (the reform movement) can be expected to move in this direction. These organizations have already shown a willingness to break ranks with the Conference of Presidents and AIPAC; in response to the peace initiative it is reasonable to expect that they will finally cross the line and call for testing the sincerity of the new state. This will mean a call for contact, for negotiations, and at the very least some measure of troop withdrawal.

Within the United States, moves of this sort on the part of

liberal mainstream Jewish organizations will be supported by large numbers of American Jews. They will also be supported by many Jewish leaders in Congress. The lock-grip that AIPAC and the Conference of Presidents has had on U.S. policy will be broken.

Moreover, there is no reason to conclude in advance that even AIPAC and the Conference of Presidents will be adamantly opposed to American policies to test and explore the true depth of the peace initiative, especially if the initiative meets with a receptive response within the Israeli mainstream. And there is no reason to think it will not. Many Israelis will be deeply skeptical, of course; and for many peace is not the issue. Thus, the Shamirs and Sharons simply want the territory, period. But many others will come forth with an open hand; perhaps Ezar Weisman will be the first; perhaps it will be Abba Eban; perhaps it will be a new generation of leaders sweeping away the Pereses and Rabins. It is not possible to say at this moment.

But if anyone is so cynical about Israeli society to doubt that the peace initiative will produce dramatic transformations, he or she should consider the significance of some of what we have already witnessed since the Uprising began. Two processes stand out. One is the increased willingness of those in the Israeli peace movement to make direct contact with Palestinians in the territories. The other is the emergence of very high-ranking military officers, some retired and some still in service, as proponents of the thesis that Israel's national security would be best served by withdrawal from the territories.

In *The New York Times* of May 31, 1988, it was reported that "a group of several dozen retired senior Israeli military officers are advocating an end to Israel's occupation of the West Bank and the Gaza Strip." A leader of the group, Major General Ori Orr, was quoted as saying, "we all agree that the occupation should end because maintaining it does more damage to our security than ending it."

And in August 1988, the Tel Aviv based International Center for Peace in the Middle East (ICPME), an organization that lists Abba Eban at the top of its letterhead, put forward a proposal for an Israeli response should a Palestinian government-in-exile be established. The ICPME proposed that the government of Israel should recognize and negotiate with the Palestinian government-in-exile provided that the Palestinian government met the following conditions:

–it recognized Israel and its right to exist;

–it declared an intention to end the conflict and sign a comprehensive treaty with Israel;

–it declared its willingness to negotiate on open borders, to demilitarize the Palestinian state, and to prevent entry of a foreign army.

That this could occur within the pre-state political framework foreshadows the enormous response there would be to a peace initiative by the new state. And this, of course, would be reflected in the attitudes of American Jews and of the United States government. This is not to say that the Israeli government will immediately sit down with representatives of the Palestinian state. But the peace initiative will create an environment in which it is not possible for the Israeli government to use its full military power to block the emergence of the Palestinian state, an environment in which the Palestinian campaign to create an Israeli willingness to withdraw can gradually grow in strength.

Democracy

As soon as its existence is declared, the new State of Palestine should also declare that it is and will remain a democracy. The leadership of the new state, the provisional government, will be provisional pending the possibility of holding national elections. Such elections should be held under the auspices of the United Nations, and an effort should be made through the United Nations to get the Israelis to permit elections even prior to troop withdrawal.

If elections could be held, they would establish the legitimacy of the elected leadership and pave the way for face-to-face negotiations with Israel. It is almost inconceivable that any Israeli government could refuse to sit down with the elected leadership of the Palestinian population. To refuse would be to refuse to sit down with anyone, for no Palestinian and no Arab leader could negotiate in the place of an elected leadership. Even without elections, the PLO has won something close to this exclusive right, though its hold on this right is periodically tested. But it is one thing to be viewed in the Arab world as the legitimate representative of the Palestinian people; it is very different when that is how a Palestinian leadership is perceived in Israel and in the United States.

Of course, these considerations would not be lost on Israeli hard-liners, and the demand for free national elections would be resisted strongly by those who continue to hold out some hope of retaining control of the territories. But the force of the appeal to permit elections is very strong and will gain many adherents. The Israelis might reasonably argue that they cannot allow elections to positions within the government of the new state since they do not recognize the existence of the state. In response, the Israelis could be asked simply to permit elections to establish which leaders speak for the Palestinians.

There are other very powerful reasons why it is critical that the new State of Palestine proclaim itself a democracy. For one, this will give added weight to the belief that the new state can and will live at peace with Israel. A government that serves at the will of the Palestinian population will have to be responsive to the desires of that population. If the new state were to become an adventurer in pursuit of maximalist Palestinian dreams, the ordinary people of the West Bank and Gaza would suffer the most. It is they who would die in a conflict, and they who would be made stateless refugees. In short, the logic of the two-state peace is that the Palestinians would have something to lose. This logic is strengthened when the people who would lose the most are the ones who select the government.

This is not some rarefied point of political science; it is something ordinary people understand in their gut. Thus, the prospect that the State of Palestine would be a democracy would immediately translate into increased confidence that a road to lasting peace had opened. This perception will be strengthened by an additional consideration: it is almost unknown for two democracies to wage war on each other. Thus, given Israeli democracy, Palestinian democracy will mean increased security for both sides.

Regardless of any Israeli response, it is essential that the new government push ahead with the establishment of democratic institutions. As mentioned earlier, the Palestine National Council will become the legislative body of the new government. Steps should be taken to broaden and publicize the democratic character of the provisional legislature as it emerges from the PNC. For instance, since the State of Palestine will permit dual citizenship, it would actually be possible to have some form of elections in which Palestinians outside the West Bank and Gaza, be they in Lebanon, the Gulf States, or the United States, vote to select some component of the provisional government. To heighten the legitimacy and political clout of such elections, they should be supervised by the United Nations.

Within the West Bank and Gaza, efforts should be made to pursue democratic forms wherever possible. This might involve secret elections or secret referendums on key issues of local policy and tactics. Because so much of the functioning of the new state will occur on the local level, there is no need for secret elections covering the entire territory. What is needed is some form of popular decision-making in each village. Moreover, inside the underground command, where secrecy has already been successfully maintained, democratic procedures should be initiated if they do not already exist.

An additional benefit of making the new State of Palestine a fledgling democracy is that this will help it gain support in the United States. This is not merely a matter of public sentiment. The new state will be accused of being a future vassal of the Soviet Union. To those familiar with Palestinian resistance to any outside authority, such charges may seem absurd. But there is no doubt that they will be made and believed. As stated earlier, this will be especially so if the Soviet Union takes the lead in providing formal recognition of the new state. That the creation of the State of Palestine will mean the addition of one more democracy to the region will go a considerable way toward dispelling these anxieties. And these anxieties are themselves relevant to the peace issue, for it will be claimed that if the State of Palestine does become a Soviet client state, then over time the Soviets might provide it with weaponry to threaten Israel.

On this issue, as with the peace initiative in general, there is no room for ploys and maneuvers. No government will have ever played to a more skeptical audience and to a more mobilized public relations opposition than will the State of Palestine. The only possibility it has of convincing the world of the sincerity of its efforts with respect both to democracy and to peace in general will rest in that sincerity itself. Thus, in carrying out a strategy along these lines, it will be crucial that the Palestinians are deeply committed to building this kind of society, not merely as a means to other ends, but for its own sake.

To many critics of the PLO such ideas seem the ultimate in fantasy. Yet I would argue that the evidence is convincing that a democratic society is in fact a genuine Palestinian aspiration, not just on the level of the average person, but inside the PLO as well.

The PLO Covenant makes no mention of a Palestinian state. That objective was formulated in 1969 when Arafat became the chairman of the PLO executive committee. At that time, the proposed Palestinian state was to be a base from which the Palestinians would be able to carry forth their struggle to "liberate" all of Palestine, i.e., to destroy the State of Israel. Over the two intervening decades this objective of an independent state as a base for struggle against Israel has been transformed into a search for the two-state solution. A great deal of the debate about the "true" nature of the PLO and the reasonableness of Israel's agreeing to the establishment of a Palestinian state turns on the question of the reality and staying power of this transformation. Many opponents of a Palestinian state are either unaware of the major transformations that have occurred both within PLO positions and in the attitudes of Palestinians, or they fear that over time there might be new transformations of a more militant kind.

Interestingly, through the twenty years of PLO evolution regarding the nature of the Palestinian state, one fixed element has been its democratic character. Thus, when the demand for an independent state was first articulated by the PLO in 1969, the central committee of Fatah issued a statement which read:

> The Fatah Palestinian National Liberation Movement is not fighting the Jews as an ethnic or religious community. It is fighting against Israel, the expression of a colonization based on a racist and expansionist technocratic system, the expression of Zionism and colonialism. . . . The Fatah Palestinian National Liberation Movement solemnly declares that the ultimate objective of its struggle is the restoration of an independent and *democratic* Palestinian state in which all citizens, of whatever religion, will enjoy equal rights.[10]

Ideologically, there has never been any challenge to the notion that the Palestinian state would be a democracy. This is not surprising. As a mixture of Moslems, Druze, Christians, and atheists, the PLO certainly could not support a theocracy. While it contained Marxist groups under its umbrella, its non-Marxist elements certainly would not support a Leninist state. Moreover, it is the non-Marxist Fatah which is the dominant group. And as none of the groups support any kind of traditional oligarchy, there is no reason to think that the PLO's intention of establishing a democratic state has been anything other than genuine.

What one might wonder is whether, good intentions aside, a Palestinian state emerging under former PLO leaders would in fact be or remain a democracy. For instance, the numerous assassinations that have occurred inside the PLO might point to a political culture intolerant of dissent. On the other hand, there are good reasons for believing that a Palestinian state would be a democracy. Here are ten:

1. Ideologically the Palestinian movement has been committed to democracy.

2. Almost all Palestinians embrace this objective.

3. The PLO leadership, especially Arafat, enjoys overwhelming popular support and, as the likely winners in any open elections, would not fear elections.

4. The high level of education achieved among Palestinians and the existence of numerous independent Palestinian institu-

tions and professional societies support democratic government.

5. Within the PLO and within constituent groups such as Fatah, democratic forms have developed, and no leader, even Arafat, has had unchecked power within the organization.

6. The Palestinians have an indirect familiarity with democracy in virtue of their proximity to Israel; they have had contact with fellow Palestinians who are Israeli citizens and have been participating, to varying degrees, in Israeli political life for the last forty years.

7. The establishment of the state will come about through the activization of the entire masses of the population, thus giving birth to a continuing demand for participation.

8. Without an army, the Palestinian state will lack a powerful military capable of seizing and holding power.

9. Palestinian society has significant experience with democratic forms on the local level; some of its most respected leaders are the elected mayors of Palestinian villages and cities, many of whom were deposed by the Israelis.

10. The national security interests of the State of Palestine would be enhanced by a democratic form of government, as this would contribute to worldwide support.

For all these reasons, it is reasonable to expect that the Palestinian state will be a democracy. One cannot rule out alternatives, even the possibility that continued struggle with Israel will give sufficient power to Islamic fundamentalism to open the door for an Islamic state. But one can be reasonably sure that even if the democratic character of the Palestinian state is challenged, the supporters of democracy will not readily give up the struggle. They will not have come this far only to be subjected to some form of authoritarian rule.

Notes: Chapter 3

[1]Discussions I had with PLO leaders in Tunis in August 1988 indicated that they saw the PLO moving into the status of a political party rather than simply going out of existence. The important point is that as the authoritative spokesman for Palestinian nationalism it must be supplanted by the government of the State of Palestine.

[2]The parallel point can be made about the need for the Israelis to take full cognizance of Palestinian needs. In part this will involve security matters, but at bottom the key to dealing with the Palestinians is mutuality. They need to be treated with respect. From the start the state building project of the Zionist movement acted as if the Palestinians simply were not there. For a long time, it was maintained that there was no Palestinian people, and even today there is a refusal to negotiate with their leadership. We will never know how different the history might have been if the Palestinians had been treated as the full bearers of moral claims. I do not dwell on these issues because this book is essentially a strategy for Palestinian action in the face of continued Israeli obtuseness.

[3]Sadat's visit was more thoroughly choreographed than is generally known.

[4]The foreign aid issue is very complex. To actually cut off aid to Israel, even if possible, would probably be counterproductive. It would convince Israelis that they were being abandoned, and might result in a decrease in moderation on the part of the Palestinians and the Arab states.

[5]Andrea Baron, "Focus on Jews and Israel," *The Washington Report on Middle East Affairs, June 1988, p. 16.*

[6]*The Washington Post,* June 2, 1988, p. A 31.

[7]"PNC Resolutions," *Israel and Palestine Political Report*, No. 133, May 1987, p. 18.

[8]I participated in one such meeting in June 1987, and Arafat

specifically made the point that affecting Israeli public opinion is the main objective. He seemed to look toward both diplomatic initiatives and armed struggle as a means of doing this. This meeting is discussed in some detail in *The Washington Report on Middle East Affairs*, September 1987.

[9]In June 1988, a U.S. court blocked the closing of the observer mission on the grounds that it would violate the United Nations Headquarters Agreement and that the Congress had not intended to do so.

[10]*International Documents on Palestine 1970*, as quoted in Alain Gresh, *The PLO: The Struggle Within*, (London: Zed Books, 1985), p. 17.

Chapter 4
CONFRONTING THE STRATEGY:
COMMON QUESTIONS

The strategy articulated in the preceding chapter raises literally hundreds of questions in a wide variety of areas. This includes matters of abstract theory, impacts on the PLO, alternative options, possible Israeli countermoves, and the roles of other actors. In the present chapter I have tried to anticipate and answer the most important questions that arise. Implicit in the questions I have selected and the answers I have given is my background analysis of the dynamics of the Israeli-Palestinian conflict.

Theory

Question: Aren't you just playing with words when you say that the state will exist? After all, a state doesn't exist just because someone stands on a soap box and says it does.

It is correct that a state doesn't exist merely by virtue of someone saying that it does. But there are many things the saying of which is part of what it is to bring them into existence. Reflect on how a marriage comes into existence. At least in some societies, when two people exchange vows and the appropriate person pronounces them married, they thereby are married. Or reflect on how any informal organization comes into existence. Five people sit around and say, "Let's form a club. Not tomorrow, not next week, but now." If all assent, if all leave the room believing they have formed a club, then in fact they have. Now, a state is neither a marriage nor a club, but it is a social form, and to some extent its being is similar to that of marriages and clubs.

Another way of looking at it is to imagine that the State of Palestine had already existed and functioned just like any other state. Then one day the country of Palestine was invaded and occupied by the Israeli army. The people refused to assent to Israeli authority; they disobeyed at every turn. Imagine then that the leadership of the state has not been captured; they meet in secret and consider three alternatives. As the first alternative they simply give up the state and go abroad as individuals. They tell all state officials that the state is defunct (like a corporation that has gone bankrupt and ceases to exist); they tell everyone to haul down the flag. They endorse protest inside the occupied territory and form groups to carry on actions outside.

As the second alternative, the government leaders abandon any effort to continue functioning within the territory, but they call themselves a government-in-exile and as a group emerge outside the territory, claiming to be the rightful authorities who should be governing.

As the third alternative, seeing the refusal of the people to accept foreign authority, they decide to go underground, not as individuals but as a state. A few key individuals would leave the country and would continue to function in international diplomacy, recognized by most of the world as representatives of the government. Inside the territory, but underground, state officials would continue to function as best they could. The flag would still be flown, the currency would still be used, the laws would be respected, and crimes would be punished. With the cooperation of the people, bit by bit they would force the Israelis to withdraw.

These are three real alternatives. And one can understand the advantages of the third alternative over the first two. The basic theory of the strategy I have proposed is that the third situation can be created, not by retreating from an already existing state, but by going forward from where the Palestinians are now, building momentum in the process.

The Decision Facing the PLO

Question: How would the strategy affect the PLO? How would it change the relationship between the leadership and the resistance within the territories?

The strategy calls for the PLO to be supplanted by a provisional government, so the PLO ceases to exist or at least fades into the background. But many of the same leaders would, no doubt, be the leaders of the new state. As such their situation would change significantly. First, the strategy provides a central role for the leadership in relation to the resistance. As is well known, the Uprising of 1988 was not planned or run from Tunis. The Uprising radically shifted the center of gravity and decision-making to those inside the territories. This is not to say that the PLO is not in charge, but rather that there is a difference between being inside and being outside the West Bank and Gaza.

Throughout the first ten months of the Uprising the diplomatic strategy coming out of Tunis was not organically linked to the efforts of the people in the territories. The working assumption has been that the Uprising puts pressure on the United States to move Israel toward an international conference and toward acceptance of a Palestinian state. But in a sense those in Tunis and those within the territory have been on two tracks which, they hope, are mutually supportive.

Those outside have felt some pressure to demonstrate that there is still some important role for them to play in relation to the Uprising. Thus, there were a series of attempted efforts to infiltrate Israel, either from the Sinai or from Lebanon. Most of these have been detected at early stages and the Palestinians involved have been killed. The attack on the bus in the Negev near Dimona in early 1988 stands out as an exception. Yet it illustrates the problem well. In operational terms the raiders were a bit more "successful" in that they actually made contact with Israeli society; but whatever the original plan, the operation degenerated into a terrorist attack on a civilian bus. In political terms the action was counterproductive. Yet it was very popular inside the territories, at least with young people in the streets. It is not the kind of operation that Arafat would have sanctioned or wanted to be identified with prior to the Uprising, for it undermines his larger diplomatic and political project. It is symptomatic of the sense of isolation from the action that those who for twenty years have been at its center must feel, that they are reduced to playing to the crowd.

The strategy serves an important internal function. It reunifies the two poles of Palestinian action, by redefining the Uprising in terms of the larger strategic role played by the PLO leadership in Tunis. The declaration of the state and the creation of the provisional government transform the Uprising from an expression of protest and resistance to a stage in the process of building the state. Thus the political and diplomatic role of the Tunis leadership provides definition for the entire Palestinian effort.

Second, so long as the Uprising remains on the level of protest and resistance it is in a vulnerable position. Pure protest and unstructured resistance cannot last forever. Moreover, so long as these efforts are understood strategically as a contribution to bringing about the hoped-for international conference, the Uprising is dependent on the continued credibility of that alternative. Once it becomes clear either that the conference is not going to take place, or that it will not produce the desired outcome, the Uprising will be seen as having failed in its larger purpose. And when that happens it is likely to degenerate into despair, terrorism, or quietism. The declaration of the existence of the state provides a long-term future for the Uprising. It gives it the task of actually bringing the existence and functioning of that state into being. And in focusing on Israeli troop withdrawal, it gives the Uprising a long-term objective against which to test and develop itself.

Events will move in the direction I am advocating, not primarily because of the power of argument, but because the strategy is to a considerable extent an outgrowth of a natural tendency within the Uprising itself. What made the Uprising what it is, was its total support by the Palestinian population. Once this was achieved, Israeli governing authority was of necessity broken. The next stage is to replace it with a new government, and the underground command is that government in embryonic form. This same tendency, which results in the declaration of the state, is captured in the way young Palestinians have come to refer to their villages as "liberated villages." It is not really the villages that have been liberated, but the villagers. But the projection of this reality onto the villages mirrors the way in which the existence of the state is constituted by the beliefs, actions, and identities of the population.

Question: The peace initiative calls upon the PLO to offer to exchange ambassadors with Israel, to declare unilaterally that they are at peace with Israel, and to refrain from all acts of terrorism and all lethal attacks on Israeli soldiers. In short, it calls on them to play a variety of cards that they have up to now refused to play without reciprocal moves on the other side. Why should they do so, and what basis is there for expecting that they will?

It all depends on what kind of game you think you are engaged in. Insofar as you imagine that a state will come into being through mutual concessions, compromise, and ultimately a negotiated agreement, then there is a danger in playing your strongest cards too soon. But it is a totally different matter if you believe that a state can be created unilaterally. Then you are not in a card game at all. The peace initiative component of this plan is not undertaken primarily in order to induce parallel Israeli moves. Rather, it is a way of creating forces that will strengthen the Palestinian hand and give it the leverage to bring about Israeli withdrawal. If this model of how the state is created is accepted, then the situation is totally transformed. One makes these moves because one believes something that was not really credible earlier: that these moves create a Palestinian state.

Question: What would the strategy mean with respect to

armed struggle and the existence of the various commando groups and other organizations that make up the PLO?

The strategy calls on the provisional government to forbid any lethal attacks upon Israeli soldiers. To the extent that stones are viewed as "arms," it leaves open that limited aspect of armed struggle. This is done on pragmatic grounds. It follows the same reasoning as the Uprising and is based on the same conclusion: to engage in lethal attacks is to invite massive Israeli force and to eliminate the political and psychological advantages of fighting without real weapons.

The strategy does not call for the Palestinians to abandon their *right* to armed struggle, but to consider the wisdom of exercising that right. On the level of rights, insofar as the provisional government is not seeking to destroy the State of Israel, but rather to force an end to Israeli occupation of the West Bank and Gaza, it is hard to see why the Palestinians would not have a right to armed struggle against Israeli soldiers. This of course does not mean a right to attack innocent civilians, to engage in terrorism.

As for the various commando groups, their future is an open question. Once the PLO goes out of existence and the provisional government is formed, either the various component groups could also go out of existence (or become non-violent political organizations) or they could simply operate on their own. If the latter course is chosen, they could not be allowed to operate from the territory of the new state. This would be a matter of great importance, and the provisional government would have to be prepared to enforce this rule.

It would be unfortunate if the groups chose to continue operations from Lebanon directed against targets inside Israel. Even if such operations were directed solely against military targets, they would still tend to be perceived as terrorist attacks. Moreover, it is unlikely that a strict rule of targeting only the Israeli military could be enforced operationally. Such attacks would contribute to an unfavorable climate inside Israel and would weaken the effectiveness of the peace initiative. If the new government clearly dissociated itself from such activity and was in fact "clean," commando activity would not be fatal to the Palestinian cause, though clearly counterproductive.

The only reason for granting autonomy to the various component organizations of the PLO is simply that it may be impossible to do anything else. The PLO has always been an umbrella organization, whose component groups have retained the ability to initiate their own actions. Allowing the different groups to go their own way allows the core of the PLO, centered around Arafat, to proclaim the state, set up the provisional government, and launch the peace initiative, without occasioning a violent showdown between the factions.

Question: What happens if the strategy fails?

This all depends on why and how it fails. If it fails because ultimately the Palestinian people throw in the towel and accept permanent Israeli rule, then that is that. Without the support of the Palestinian people an independent state cannot come into being, through any route.

But if it "fails" simply because after some set period of time, Israeli troop have still not withdrawn, then who is to say that this is "failure"? One of the great strengths of a strategy focused on achieving Israeli troop withdrawal is that there is no point at which it makes sense simply to give up. So long as the strategy is followed, the continued presence of Israeli troops makes less and less sense from an Israeli point of view. As more and more time goes by, the costs of continued occupation will multiply and, given the absence of terrorism and lethal attacks on Israeli soldiers and a standing offer of negotiations, these costs will put constant pressure on the Israelis. There is no telling in advance how long it will take to produce troop withdrawal. But the strategy should be undertaken with an awareness that it could be a long time, by which I mean five to ten years.

But it is also possible for the strategy to fall apart in its implementation. Suppose that only a few states recognize the new state; suppose that Israeli government or settler provocations produce some attacks on Israeli soldiers; suppose that the commando groups continue terrorist attacks on Israeli civilians; suppose that Israeli intelligence penetrates the underground government and arrests most leaders; suppose that Israel kills Arafat and the other top leaders of the government; suppose that the level of response to any protest inside the West Bank and Gaza is so severe as to crush all mass activity. If all this were to occur the strategy would have failed. There are no guarantees. If all this comes to pass, then the situation will degenerate into a cycle of violence, terror, repression, and possibly war. It will be an open-ended catastrophe for both the Israelis and the Palestinians.

Such a catastrophe for both peoples should not be viewed as unlikely. Indeed, with the current trend of events, we may find ourselves in an unrecognizably horrible situation in a very short time. One virtue of this strategy is that it opens the door to a real alternative for both peoples. But it is merely the last best hope; it is not foolproof.

Question: Will the strategy proposal in itself have an effect?

As the strategy of unilaterally declaring the existence of the state becomes a serious alternative for the PLO, this will be well noted inside of Israel. It may generate preemptive countermoves. Thus, fairly decisive action is needed on the part of the PLO. Further, the onset of despair and random violence may be just around the corner; one can wait too long.

Another alternative is also possible: the prospect of the declaration of the state, or its actual occurrence, may prompt the Israeli government to enter just the sort of international conference that the PLO has been seeking. And the Israeli government, which would not sit down with the PLO, might be prepared to sit down with a new organization that offers mutual recognition and foreswears terrorism. If this were to occur, a contextual decision would have to be made on whether to proceed with the strategy in any event or to hold off and see what a conference generates. The fact that a strong alternative remains open if either there is no conference or the conference does not produce significant results could be a powerful incentive. My own belief, however, is that Israel is the prisoner of its own internal politics, ideologies, and mythologies, and that the Palestinians' best option is to push forward immediately.

Question: The strategy functions only if the Palestinians really accept the two-state solution and do not view an independent state as a vehicle for destroying Israel. What reason is there for believing that they have finally come to this conclusion?

If one wants to look, there is plenty of evidence that both the Palestinian leadership and the Palestinian people understand that they cannot eliminate Israel; further, they also know that once they have a state of their own, its safety will depend on their getting along with Israel. On the leadership level, Arafat has stated publicly that, "You can't get rid of the state of Israel." Since 1985 he has been actively seeking to negotiate with it. That he may harbor a more sinister dream in the recesses of his brain is possible, but largely irrelevant. The success of the strategy requires only a policy of commitment to the two-state solution. As for Israel's security, this will always rest in large measure on Israel's strength, not on trust in Palestinian intentions. However, if the Israelis meet the Palestinian peace initiative halfway, then it will be possible to build new political realities to make the peace increasingly more durable.

This issue of Palestinian desires, which constantly arises, is often misconceived. If one insists that the Palestinians convert to Zionism, that they come to believe that the creation of the State of Israel was just, then one is indeed living in a fantasy land. This will never happen. And the reason is not some kind of Palestinian obtuseness. It is based on historical realities. The Palestinians were essentially a Third World people living under colonial rule, first of the Turks and then of the British. Starting in the late nineteenth century and through the years prior to the Second World War, just as nationalism was stirring throughout the Third World and colonialism was coming to an end, they were hit by the Zionist movement which largely arrived from Europe.

Whatever one wants to say about the right of the Jewish people to establish their state in this area, either before or after the Second World War, for the Palestinians it has meant dispossession. This was especially true in 1948 when in fear, under wartime conditions, and in some instances under Israeli guns, they left or were forced from their homes and villages.[1] No people in the world would ever come to think it was just that this should happen to them. The most that can ever be hoped for is that the Palestinians would appreciate that the moral issues are at least complex. And even this might be too much to ask of the people who have gotten the short end of the stick. After all, there is very little recognition among Jews, either in Israel or in the United States, that the Palestinians have suffered a vast injustice. And this failure to appreciate "moral complexity" comes from a people with a very highly developed conscience, who have emerged as the victor in the struggle and thus could afford to appreciate the other side's point of view.

Whether or not, formally and as a government, Palestinians are now prepared to do things that the PLO has not yet done, remains to be seen. But the issue is always a concrete one. It depends on whether or not it actually makes sense for them to take a specific step. It is one thing to come to accept the fact that it is virtually impossible to recover land that was yours; it is something else for a government to adopt a public policy that eschews such an objective. Why should the government of Palestine take the latter step just because the leadership, as individuals, have come to accept the fact? This requires not a mere acceptance of reality, but a pragmatic decision. And the decision will be based on its pros and cons, factors which can be influenced by non-Palestinians.

Rather than sitting around and asking passively, "Are the Palestinians really ready to accept Israel?" Israel, the United States, and in particular the Jewish community need to create conditions that give the Palestinians some real incentive to make pragmatic decisions. After forty years of struggle with Israel and a hundred years of struggle with Zionism, most Palestinians want to end the conflict, but they must get a state of their own in exchange for ending it. The logic of Palestinian politics is not unusual in mitigating against unilateral concessions; unilateralism is not a common practice in international relations.

Supporters of Israel, and the Israeli government itself, need to say publicly to the Palestinian leadership, "If you do this, then this is what I will do in return. . . ." Specifically, American leaders, Israeli leaders, and Jews everywhere need to say, "If you declare the state, and if you really do take these other steps toward peace, then I will publicly support your efforts. I will call for recognition of the State of Palestine; I will meet with your representatives; I will struggle for the success of your efforts, for they shall be my efforts also."

Question: Doesn't this strategy call for a commitment to nonviolent civil disobedience? Doesn't it require a charismatic leader of the Martin Luther King or Mahatma Gandhi type? Do the Palestinians have such a leader?

They do not have such a leader, but neither do they need one. The strategy does not call on the Palestinians to make a principled commitment to nonviolence. Indeed, it is expected that some violent confrontations with Israeli troops on the stone-throwing model will continue.

The strategy does call for tremendous self-discipline from the Palestinian community. But this they have demonstrated already in the Uprising. Broadly speaking the strategy is only an extension of the Uprising. It builds on forms and styles and strengths that are already present. Furthermore, it is important to realize that the civil disobedience aspects of the strategy, like those of the Uprising, are really quite different from what civil disobedience came to mean in the U.S. civil rights movement. Martin Luther King made no challenge to the basic legitimacy of the government; he challenged specific laws that he found unjust and inconsistent with our Constitution. He willingly accepted the legal consequences of doing so. In some instances civil disobedience was not even directed at an unjust law, but was used to call attention to some problem or unjust practice. Thus, one might sit-in at the courthouse in violation of a law that one otherwise accepts, in order to awaken the conscience of the nation to the exclusion of blacks from juries.

Although this dimension exists in the Palestinian struggle, the real meaning of civil disobedience tactics here lies in their challenge to the very existence of the Israeli administration. It is the fact of Israeli rule that the Palestinians in the West Bank and Gaza are rebelling against; theirs is not essentially a civil rights struggle; it is a political revolution of a subject people against foreign rulers. They are largely limited to non-lethal means because of the permanent reality of the disparity of power.

Question: Can the Palestinians simply adopt part of the strategy, say the declaration of the existence of the state, and reject others, say the peace initiative?

This could be done, but it would be a tragic mistake. The declaration of the existence of the state and the adoption of the state-building strategy will serve important functions. They will allow for a worldwide diplomatic offensive and extend the life of the Uprising. They will accomplish some of this even without the peace initiative.

However, to forego the peace initiative is to cripple the effectiveness of the strategy and to expose the Palestinian people to serious risks. As stated earlier, the peace initiative is what will help create conditions inside Israel and inside the United States that will protect the new state from draconian measures against it. It is what will ultimately make Israeli withdrawal possible. So while the state can be declared without the peace initiative, such a declaration would be irresponsible.

Question: Is there some point at which it would make sense for the Palestinians to open a campaign of lethal violence against either settlers or soldiers in the West Bank or Gaza?

No. This will be and will continue to be exactly what the extremists in Israel would like to see happen. The use of lethal violence will give them the opportunity they need. And it will serve no purpose. It is simply impossible to force the Israelis out through violent methods. Any group attempting this from inside the territories will have to be stopped in its tracks.

It may not be easy for everyone concerned to understand and accept this. The temptation to use lethal means will remain a constant danger point; top priority in implementing the strategy must be given to maintaining discipline on this score.

Israeli Interests

Question: Why should any friend of Israel support this strategy?

First, if a strategy of this sort is not implemented, we will soon be faced with a spiral of violence that will ultimately lead to another war.

Second, this strategy can bring about the two-state solution. The argument for the two-state solution is simply that it is more desirable for Israel than any of the other alternatives. Although many of the reasons for this conclusion have already been addressed, they need to be reiterated in this context:

–A two-state solution will be widely accepted by the Arab world, by Palestinians, and by the PLO or provisional government. Thus it will have staying power.

–It will provide symmetry. The Jews have a state, and the Palestinians will have a state. Any other alternative is so far from being fair that future generations of Palestinians are bound to reopen the issue.

–Giving the Palestinians a state of their own gives them something to lose; allowing the PLO to evolve into the government of this state allows them to take on the responsibility of protecting their population and the survival of their state. It is this, and Israeli military power, which will ensure that a Palestinian state will not become a base for attacks on Israel.

–Giving up the territories will solve the so-called

"demographic problem." Israel will not be faced with ruling over lands in which a majority of the population is non-Jewish.

–The two-state solution will cement the peace with Egypt and result in a peace treaty with Jordan.

–The two-state solution will focus Palestinian energies on building their own society. It will temper the extent to which the overthrow of King Hussein becomes the outlet for Palestinian nationalism.

–If there is a demilitarized Palestinian state, in the event of some future threat to Israel from Arab states, Israeli forces would be able to secure the strategic points in the West Bank and Gaza overnight.

Question: Why will the Israelis withdraw?

The Israelis will withdraw because they will come to perceive that it is in their interest, all things considered, to do so. Already, leading military experts in Israel are calling for withdrawal. If this strategy is pursued, these voices will become louder. It is possible that Israeli troops might withdraw at an early stage, essentially giving the two-state solution a chance. It is more likely that they will only withdraw at a later point, when it is clear that the peace initiative is genuine, when there is a worldwide call for them to withdraw, and when the costs of continued occupation are substantial.

Question: What risks does this strategy pose for the Israelis?

The strategy calls on the Israelis to do something very difficult: to give up territories they have come to regard as their own. Today, after over twenty years of occupation, most Israelis have no memory of any time at which they did not rule over the Arab population of the West Bank and Gaza. Israelis, like all people, tend to experience what is familiar as what is right. Young Israelis have been taught that these lands are theirs. Thus it will be a wrenching experience to yield them. It is this, rather than any risks to Israel, which is the main problem.

On the security side, the possibility remains that once a Palestinian state comes into being, it will arm itself and seek to destroy Israel. Such possibilities cannot be ruled out. But these risks are low, and Israel will have adequate means at her disposal for dealing with them. The real danger is that she may perceive threats where none exist.

It must also be remembered that over time Israel could find herself in a far less attractive position in the Middle East. Today Jordan and Egypt are ruled by moderate governments; Lebanon remains in chaos; Syria is militarily inferior to Israel; the Arab states have floundering economies and enormous internal problems; the Iran-Iraq conflict is not yet resolved; Israel retains a nuclear monopoly; the Soviet Union remains committed to Israel's right to exist; Islamic fundamentalism has not gained widespread support among the Palestinians. In short, Israel is in a position of relative strength. It can reasonably be assumed that some of these factors will shift against Israel over time. Israel is much better served by reaching a peace settlement on the desirable terms it can achieve now than by facing a continued conflict into the indefinite future.

It might be argued that, since Israel's military strength relative to the Arab states will probably decline, it is important for it to hold every military asset it can. Several things are wrong with this analysis. First, whatever value the West Bank and Gaza have as military assets could be regained through an Israel preemptive move if war ever seemed imminent. Israel could probably negotiate a settlement with the Palestinians to facilitate this. Monitoring devices could be installed in advance; basic defensive positions could be designated as special zones that were closed to all parties; Israeli air cavalry could be developed for exactly such a mission, and so forth. But more basically, national security, especially in the age of chemical and nuclear weapons, rests on the ability to avoid war. Avoiding war is a matter of reducing the causes of war and of maintaining a strong deterrent. Israel already has all the deterrent it will ever need; at bottom, its nuclear capacity alone ensures that it can totally destroy any enemy even if this means its own destruction. The great weakness in the Israeli national security framework is not on the military side but on the political side.

Israel has not accomplished much toward reducing the causes of war. Many of the most prestigious Israeli intelligence and military experts understand this, but they cannot overcome the determination of the Israeli right-wing to hold onto the territories. Within Israel at least the debate is wide open. The great irony is that in the United States, any Israeli government policy receives the empty-headed but passionate support of much of the leadership of the American Jewish establishment. What we really need in this country is a no-holds-barred debate in the Jewish community over how to promote Israeli national security. The refrain "leave it to the Israelis" misses the main point: Israeli positions vis-à-vis the Palestinians are not made on the basis of a national security analysis. They emerge from the turmoil of internal Israeli politics.

Question: What if a Palestinian state lays claim to the territories that Israel gained in the 1948 war, but were not allotted to it in the 1947 Partition Plan?

There are no permanent guarantees in international affairs. No matter what is agreed upon and appears settled, someone can always raise the "what if" question. What if Mexico one day becomes powerful and demands the return of California? What if the Soviet Union someday says that the Czar was cheated and wants Alaska back?

It is not that such hypotheticals are absurd. Some are and some are not. It is rather that the response to them consists not in showing that they could not happen, but in taking steps to ensure that they do not. Or to ensure that if they do happen, they are not serious problems. One aspect of this is military strength, but enough has already been said on that score. A variety of political factors suggests that the issue of claims to areas such as the Galilee will be manageable, if they ever arise at a later date:

–The Arab citizens of Israel experience themselves as Palestinians but also as Israeli citizens. They have no desire to leave

Israel and become instead citizens of a Palestinian state. Their first commitment is to their land and cities. The depth of their loyalty to Israel is affected by two main issues, the extent to which they see Israel as an oppressor of their Palestinian cousins in the West Bank and Gaza, and the extent to which they are permitted full entry into Israeli society. A settlement providing for a Palestinian state would reduce the tension of their dual identity as Palestinians and Israeli citizens.

In addition, in the event of a settlement, Israeli Arabs (who constitute a significant minority) will become a much more potent political force as their support will be sought by all political parties. At present, they vote for the Labor Party, the Communist Party, or for smaller parties. There is no serious competition between Likud and Labor for the Arab vote. Remaining citizens of Israel has attractions for Arabs; if Israel becomes a better place for them to live, these attractions will grow.

–A comprehensive settlement along the two-state idea would transform Arab relations with Israel. If it is accepted by the Palestinians, it will be accepted by Arabs everywhere. If at some later date, future generations of Palestinians seek to reopen these issues, they will not be able to count on automatic Arab support.

–Once a settlement is reached, a wide variety of alternative political and economic linkages will be possible for Israel, Palestine, and Jordan. A range of options, including economic union, political federation, and multiple citizenship, will create a new political environment. On this score, one might return again to a passage from the Israeli Declaration of Independence:

> The STATE OF ISRAEL will be ready to cooperate with the organs and representatives of the United Nations in the implementation of the Resolution of the Assembly of November 29, 1947, and will take steps to bring about the Economic Union over the whole of Palestine.

If the idea of economic union between two independent states was taken seriously when the two-state solution was the common wisdom, it can also be taken seriously when the two-state solution becomes a reality.

So while one can never rule out the possibility that the status of the Galilee be reopened in the future, Israel is capable of dealing with the problem, militarily if it has to, but preferably through a reawakened awareness that a sound foreign policy also consists of creativity in the political and economic sphere.

Finally, it should be remembered that these "what if" questions can be asked of any proposed solution. What if Israel expels the Palestinians, and some day the Arab countries are stronger than Israel? What if they give the territory back to Jordan and there is a Palestinian revolution in Jordan, and then there is a claim on the Galilee? Is that a more attractive prospect?

The Role of Other Actors

Question: What role does the United States play in this strategy?

The proposed strategy takes the initiative for achieving a peaceful settlement in the Middle East away from the United States and gives it to the Palestinians. The strategy can move forward with no cooperation from the U.S. government. Up to this point, PLO strategy has relied heavily on the Americans. After all, given the proposition that a Palestinian state can be created only with prior Israeli agreement, the obvious fact that the Israelis are deeply opposed to such a state leads to the search for some way of forcing their agreement. It is on the Americans that the PLO has rested its hopes. Although this seems naive, this has been the main logic of the international conference strategy. In saying this, I am not maintaining that the PLO has put its faith in American good intentions or in America's sense of justice; rather, it has believed that it could create a situation in which American interests would compel the United States to apply the necessary pressure on Israel.

The mistake in this assumption was not in thinking that it would be in America's interest to support a Palestinian state. The two-state solution will bring a stable peace to the region; it will go a long way toward creating a more secure political environment for U.S. allies (e.g., Egypt and Jordan); it will reduce the very serious possibility of another Arab-Israeli war, with its great danger of dragging the superpowers into a nuclear confrontation; and it will remove a major factor behind anti-American sentiment in the region.

The PLO has also been correct on a second point, that by intensifying the threats to American interests it could propel U.S. policy into action. This is exactly what the Uprising accomplished. For five years, the Reagan Administration largely turned its back on the Israeli-Palestinian conflict. Then within weeks after the beginning of the Uprising, Secretary of State George Shultz was making it one of his top priorities. A major factor in this transformation was the fear that the Uprising would give rise to instability in Egypt and Jordan. This possibility was made clear by the leaders of those countries themselves.

The great weakness in the PLO analysis has been the belief that if a) you activated the United States, and b) a two-state solution was in American interests, then c) you could activate U.S. policy sharply in the direction of a two-state solution. This has not happened, and under present conditions it is unlikely to happen. Such hopes are based on an inadequate model of U.S. foreign policy formulation. It treats the United States as a black box that can be fine-tuned in its behavior by affecting it from the outside; what it ignores is the overriding importance of American internal politics as a determinant of U.S. policy.

American policy in the Middle East is shaped to a great extent by the climate of opinion in the American Jewish community, which in turn is to a considerable extent a function of the views and uniformity of opinion within Israel. Thus a precondition for American support for the two-state solution is that at least some important segment of Israeli public opinion and political leadership must support it. It does not have to be Israeli government policy; the United States has not completely ceded its foreign policy to Israeli leaders. The United States government can break ranks with the Israeli government; but it cannot ignore the entire spectrum of mainstream opinion within Israel.

In relation to the proposed strategy, the U.S. reaction can range from deep opposition to Palestinian statehood at the one extreme to recognition of the new state at the other. Where the United States ends up along this spectrum will not be a question of who is in the White House, but primarily a question of the state of American public opinion, especially Jewish public opinion. In fact, recent polls indicate that most Americans are favorably disposed to the idea of a Palestinian state. However, it is not polls that matter, but rather organized political forces with a passionate interest. Where the American Jewish community comes out, and whether it is unified or deeply divided, will depend on how adequately the provisional government pursues the peace initiative.

If the United States wants to play a constructive role, then there are many critical functions it can undertake:

–It can lay a restraining hand on Israel, basically preventing Israel from adopting any draconian tactics such as transfer, or destruction of the Palestinian economy.

–It can open contact (even if it delays recognition) with the officials of the new government. This would help them achieve worldwide legitimacy and would reinforce those within the provisional government most committed to the peace initiative.

–Even prior to the declaration of independence and statehood, the United States could signal the PLO that it would respond well to the declaration and the peace initiative. This could prove very significant in the PLO's evaluations of its options.

–Once the strategy is adopted, the United States could conditionally commit itself to a major assistance program for the new country. The prospect of strong American assistance and friendship on the one hand would be supportive of the strategy and, on the other, would help to allay Israeli fears about having a hostile new state on its borders.

–The U.S. government, with the right kind of leadership, could also play a valuable role in shaping public opinion both within Israel and the United States. It could call public attention to the great opportunities for lasting peace if Israel responds favorably to the peace initiative. It could support the call for nationwide Palestinian elections and urge Israeli leaders to test Palestinian sincerity.

–At a later stage, the United States can take steps to help address key issues that may ultimately become important topics for Israeli-Palestinian negotiations, such as the right to return (e.g., the United States could offer Palestinians in Lebanon an opportunity to become U.S. citizens and the U.S. could take the leadership in establishing a fund to compensate Palestinians for lost lands).

–Finally, the United States can help counter Israeli and Jewish-American fears for Israel's security, by indicating a willingness to enter into a formal defense pact with Israel if Israel were to accept a Palestinian state. I suggest this not because I believe it necessary for Israeli security, and I do not wish to contribute to the myth of the Palestinian threat. But it may be useful as one additional security blanket. Indeed, perhaps the United States should even go further. It mollifies the fears of our NATO allies by having the "trip wire" of American troops in Europe; in the context of a full Middle Eastern settlement it could offer to do the same for the Israelis.

At the same time, however, a United States that is deeply hostile to the new state of Palestine could provide an environment within which Israeli leaders would feel emboldened to take decisive military steps to crush it. Thus it should be clear that while the strategy displaces the United States as the center of action, it does not and cannot remove the United States as a key player.

Question: What role can the Soviet Union play?

The Soviet response will be very important in several respects:

–Soviet support for the new state will help it gain worldwide legitimacy.

–Soviet support will affect the attitudes of certain Arab states, most importantly Syria.

–Soviet support will in one way or another affect the American role. On the one hand, the United States would not want to give the Soviets the advantage of being the great supporter of the new state with the United States cast in the role of the great opponent. On the other hand, if it looks as if the new state will be allied too closely to the Soviet Union, this may create pressures within the U.S. government to try to block the state from emerging. This in turn will be affected by the general tenor of U.S.–Soviet relations.

Question: What about Syria?

Relations with Syria have to be thought through very carefully. Potentially, Syria may be the one state with the most to lose from the strategy. Syria seeks to regain the Golan Heights, territory it lost in the 1967 war. At the very least, it would like to see the Heights demilitarized. At present, Israeli forces have a straight shot at Damascus, only an hour away in a speeding tank.

The Syrians thus see the Israeli-Palestinian conflict as a means for exerting some leverage over Israel. The prospect of an Israeli-Palestinian settlement will confront the Syrians with the possibility of being truly left out in the cold. Thus, if there is a settlement, Israel will achieve peace with the Palestinians, Jordan, and Egypt. This would mean the failure of the long thrust of Syrian policy since the "betrayal" by Sadat.

In turn, the Syrians are a powerful factor. They have considerable influence with some factions of the PLO; they have some supporters within the West Bank and Gaza; and they have the decisive role in Lebanon, where several hundred thousand Palestinians live in refugee camps and where Islamic fundamentalist groups with deep hostility to Israel continue to expand their influence.

Syrian efforts to be a "spoiler" must be taken seriously. One particular Syrian strategy would be to foster a cycle of violence that would prevent a positive Israeli response to the peace initiative and might provoke the Israelis into a major military move within the territories. This could be pursued by stepped-up terrorist attacks in Europe, inside Israel, or inside the territories. Thus, the Syrians could become the de facto allies of Israeli hardliners looking for an excuse to crush the new state. The Palestinians can take steps to block Syrian moves in these directions. The total rejection of terrorism is very important in this regard. If it is the law of the new state, preventing terrorism should be made a top enforcement priority, so that no terrorist operations are organized from the West Bank and Gaza. And more generally, the seriousness of the peace initiative will help cushion reactions to acts of planned provocation.

The preferable strategy, however, is to work out some modus vivendi with the Syrians in advance. This will not be easy, because Palestinian and Syrian interests are not the same. It would be a decisive drawback to the Palestinian cause for it to be tied down to Syrian aspirations to regain the Golan Heights. What could be arranged would be Palestinian support for demilitarization of the Heights; and if the Syrians were willing, Israel could be offered the prospect of a comprehensive settlement in which it would also gain recognition from Syria.

This approach could be part of the peace initiative, if the Syrians are prepared to join in. And if they are, this in turn will give the peace initiative even more force. The Syrian position will be influenced by the attitude of the Soviets and by their own assessment of their options. It must be remembered that once the Palestinians decide to move forward with this strategy, they have very strong cards to play. Syrian attempts at a spoiler role could result in complete Syrian isolation; hence it is a two-way street.

Question: What about Egypt?

It can be expected that the Egyptians would be very supportive of both the declaration of statehood and the peace initiative. So long as the Palestinian-Israeli conflict remains an open sore, the question of whether or not Sadat, and by extension Mubarak, sold out the Palestinians to regain the Sinai remains on the table.

Massive struggle in the West Bank and Gaza threatens Egyptian political stability. To protect itself the regime must either distance itself from Israel or help bring about a settlement. This concern activated President Mubarak even before the Uprising in efforts to work out, with U.S. support, a joint Israeli-Jordanian-Egyptian-Palestinian peace effort centering around the 1985 Amman Accords signed by Arafat and King Hussein.

While Egypt would be supportive, what useful role could it play? There are two arenas in which Egypt might have some influence: in Israel and in the United States. The Egyptian-Israeli peace treaty is a central pillar of Israeli national security. So long as that treaty is solid, no combination of Arab states can pose a lethal threat to Israel. Egypt can offer the Israelis the prospect of a real flowering of Israeli-Egyptian relations if they acquiesce to the establishment of the State of Palestine. The absence of real Egyptian-Israeli friendship has always been significant to the Israelis, because it has always made the peace treaty highly vulnerable to changes in regime and in policy. The Egyptians could thus bolster the national security arguments in favor of the two-state solution by being forthcoming about the ways in which Egyptian-Israeli friendship could develop in the wake of Israeli acceptance of the Palestinian state.

The United States has made an enormous commitment to Egypt. Second only to Israel as a recipient of U.S. aid, Egypt gets over a billion dollars in assistance from the United States each year. Since it is the largest and most prestigious of the Arab nations, Egypt's relations with the United States are central to America's position in the region. The Shultz initiative demonstrates that U.S. foreign policy makers take Egyptian concerns seriously. The president of Egypt can sit down with the president of the United States and make a case for an American peace initiative. Egypt can thus play a useful role as one of a variety of influences on U.S. policy.

Question: What about Jordan?

Jordanian attitudes toward the Palestinians have always been complex. In 1948 Jordanian involvement in the war against Israel was not essentially motivated by an effort to destroy Israel.[2] Jordan was interested in gaining control of much of the territory that was to have become an independent Palestinian state. Indeed, prior to the outbreak of the 1948 war, Jordan engaged in unsuccessful but serious secret negotiations with the Israelis designed to ensure that Israeli and Jordanian forces would not engage each other. As it turned out, the territories other than the Gaza Strip that were to have been part of the Palestinian state were split between Israel and Jordan. Both countries annexed the territories that they seized. The Israeli annexation held; the Jordanian annexation was not recognized by any other country in the world.

For the nineteen years that Jordan ruled over the West Bank, no Palestinian state was allowed to emerge. Only after 1967, when Jordan lost control of the West Bank to Israel, did Jordanian attitudes toward Palestinian nationalism grow more complex. At first the PLO was a welcome or at least tolerated guest within Jordan; but in 1970, contrary to Arafat's leanings, groups within the PLO manifested their aspirations for overthrowing Hussein and establishing a Palestinian state in Jordan. This was and remains a real possibility because more than half of Jordan's population is Palestinian. Hussein turned the Jordanian Army against the PLO and, after inflicting a tremendous toll upon them, drove them into refuge in Lebanon.

In recent years Hussein's relations with the PLO have blown hot and cold. At points Hussein was basically conspiring with Israeli Prime Minister/Foreign Minister Peres to return much of the West Bank to Jordanian control. Essentially Hussein has been prepared to cooperate with the Israelis in blocking the emergence of a Palestinian state. In part this reflects his own territorial desires with respect to the West Bank, but it also reflects his quite rational concerns about whether or not such a state would seek his own overthrow.

At the same time, and it may grow in attractiveness over time, there is the Sharon solution. This involves overthrowing Hussein and allowing a Palestinian state to emerge in Jordan. Israel would retain control over the West Bank, and the Palestinians could either live under continued Israeli rule or abandon their land and move to Jordan. While such events would mean that Israel would be exchanging the essentially benign King Hussein for a militant Palestinian state on its borders (and one that would not be a demilitarized mini-state sandwiched between Israel and Jordan), such are the realities of the politics of national security inside Israel that this may yet come to pass.

Thus, if Hussein is offered the real possibility of a Palestinian mini-state with no expansionist program aimed in his direction, it is likely that he would support it given the likely alternative. The Uprising appears to have convinced Hussein that the prospect of his ever regaining control of the West Bank is nil. One can never be sure about Hussein's thinking, but recent statements indicate that he may have finally come to this conclusion.

The great role that Hussein can play is with respect to any lingering Israeli national security fears about the Palestinian state. The West Bank component of the mini-state would be completely enclosed by Israel on the one side and Jordan on the other. Hussein can, in effect, join the Palestinian peace initiative by offering Israel both a peace treaty with Jordan and a guarantee that he will do his part to ensure the demilitarization of the State of Palestine. This of course would be much in his interest; indeed, he would be far more vulnerable than Israel. Moreover, Hussein could hold open the possibility of any of a variety of plans for future economic linkages between Israel, Palestine, and Jordan.

Question: This is primarily a strategy for the Palestinians. What should Israelis and Americans concerned with peace be doing?

Actions by Israelis and Americans, especially Jewish Americans, can play a vital role in creating the conditions under which the PLO would be more inclined to adopt the strategy. The basic thing that the PLO needs to know is that an effort of this sort will be successful. A key aspect of this is the kind of response the strategy will produce inside the Jewish community in the United States and Israel. Thus, every attempt should be made to demonstrate that if the provisional government were to launch and sustain the peace initiative, it would gain the growing support of large numbers of American and Israeli Jews.

Organizations and individuals never cease generating statements and pronouncements. Most of the time they are negatives, either announcing opposition to something, or saying that something should not be done unless such and such occurs. The most typical of these in relation to the Israeli-Palestinian conflict have concerned prohibitions against talking with the PLO. It is rather striking how rare it is to find commitments to respond positively if the other side were to act accordingly. Yet PLO decision-makers are always asking the question, "What will we get in exchange if we do such and such?" Here are two examples of the kind of conditional statements for which it would be very useful to generate support:

–If a Palestinian state declares itself at peace with Israel, then Israel should withdraw from the territories.

–If the PLO converts itself into a provisional government, and offers Israel an exchange of ambassadors, then the United States should recognize the new state and urge Israel to do so as well.

In short, Jews everywhere and non-Jews as well should make clear that if they oppose a Palestinian state they do so not on principle, but out of a concern for Israeli security, and that if this concern is met, they will support the two-state solution. Organizations and individuals who come to this conclusion should then encourage elected officials to go on record with similar conditional statements. It is time to make the Palestinians an offer they cannot refuse.

Israeli Countermoves

Question: Does it matter which party is in power in Israel?

It matters a great deal. At present both Likud and Labor are firmly opposed to a Palestinian state. But the reasons for their opposition are weighted somewhat differently. The Labor Party is prepared to exchange land for peace. It does not believe that such a deal can be made with the PLO, and it appears to believe that something along those lines can be achieved with Jordan.

The Likud, on the other hand, is opposed in principle to the relinquishment of the territory.

For Shamir and Sharon the issue is not primarily national security; they are prepared to incur national security risks in order to hold onto the territory. The aspiration to make Judea and Sumaria part of Israel is part of Shamir's lifelong political identity. Thus the difference is that at least, in principle, a Labor government could be persuaded to accept a Palestinian state if–and it is a very big "if"–it could be convinced that this would give Israel real security. For Labor this would solve the problem of how Israel could remain a Jewish state and a democracy, a dilemma surely less important to most members of Likud.

On the other hand, insofar as Labor has set itself in opposition to a Palestinian state and dismisses the peace initiative as a ploy (a likely response), the tactics that Labor might employ will not be subject to any greater humanitarian constraints than those chosen by Likud. But the tactics might differ simply because of their attitudes toward the relinquishment of territory.

Question: What kinds of countermoves might be attempted?

A wide array of moves is at the disposal of an Israeli government seeking to block the full emergence of a Palestinian state. Broadly speaking they fall into three categories: 1) annexation, 2) conflict escalation, and 3) counter-settlement moves.

On the surface annexation might appear an effective step. If the Israelis make the West Bank and Gaza part of Israel, then how can they be part of some other state? Yet in fact, annexation will not work as a countermove and it will bring its own problems. One problem with annexation is the status of the Arab population if the West Bank and Gaza are annexed. If, like the other Palestinians living in Israel, they are given citizenship, Israel would soon have an Arab majority. To prevent this, Israel would have to develop two classes of citizens, thus formalizing some form of apartheid. This would not be easy to accomplish internally and would pose a permanent challenge to the moral legitimacy of Israel as a state. The prospect of placing itself in the untenable position of South Africa is not attractive.

The main problem with annexation as a countermove is that it would not stick. No country in the world would recognize these areas as part of Israel. Nor would they be recognized as such by the Palestinian population. The annexation assertion would be as hollow as that made by Hussein after the 1967 war. And support for the Palestinian claim for independence would only be strengthened globally. The provisional government would continue to press its drive for recognition and for Israeli troop withdrawal. The pressure it would be able to bring upon Israel, economically, diplomatically, and morally, would only be strengthened by formal annexation.

By "conflict escalation" I mean to include any of a variety of violent steps designed to weaken the Palestinian cause or to allow the Israelis to impose a radical military solution.

The radical military solutions include internal and external transfer measures that would strip the West Bank of its Palestinian population, as well as measures that would raise the level of punishment for the Palestinian population so high that finally all internal resistance is overwhelmed.

There should be no doubt that were Israel to use the full force of the physical power at its disposal it could carry out such measures. Thus, as mentioned earlier, it could choose to transport hundreds of thousands of Palestinians from the West Bank to Gaza; it could, under circumstances of war, invade Jordan, hold territory on the East Bank of the Jordan river and then forcibly transfer the bulk of the West Bank population into Jordan; or it could, à la El Salvador, Argentina, Chile, Syria, and many other countries, simply unleash military or para-military forces (i.e., death squads) to crush all opposition. What the world has seen and accepted from one end of the globe to another, be it in Cambodia, Indonesia, or Guatemala, should leave no one in doubt about what can be done and done quickly if there are no restraints on the exercise of military force against civilian populations.

To many people it is simply unthinkable that Israel would use such tactics. Even to raise such issues is viewed as "anti-Israeli" in much of the Jewish community in America. But if "unthinkable" has any meaning, it merely means that people do not like to think about it. To some extent, there probably already exist detailed contingency plans that would make one's hair stand up. In any event, Palestinians who experienced forced expulsion in 1948 and remember all too well Deir Yasin and Sabra and Shatila should have no illusions. Unfortunately, sometimes it appears that many Palestinians are either constitutionally unable to imagine that things can get much worse, or in spite of themselves, they have partially succumbed to Israel's forceful projection of itself as essentially benign. It is not that they do not know better; the average Palestinian child has a firmer grasp on this reality than most Jewish intellectuals in the United States. But through some strange failure of the imagination, the past does not get sufficiently projected into future possibilities.

In any event, let there be no illusions about the physical possibility of ultimate countermeasures. The real issue is the political possibility of invoking such measures. The constraints against their use are both internal and external. They have been discussed earlier and include moral scruples, fears of civil insurrection, and national security, economic, and diplomatic considerations.

The important point is that these constraints can be breached under certain conditions. These include: war with the Arab states, a major terror campaign inside Israel, or a spiral of escalating violence generated by attacks on settlers and soldiers in the West Bank and Gaza. The appropriate Palestinian countermeasures to strengthen all the constraints are contained in the peace initiative. If for some reason the Palestinians lack the will or resolve to pursue the peace initiative, then they would best be advised to forget the strategy of attempting to impose a Palestinian state unilaterally upon Israel. For without the peace initiative, they will be sitting ducks for conflict escalation. It should be remembered, however, that the peace initiative has dual purposes. Hopefully, the Israelis will grasp the hand extended to them, but even if they do not, the peace initiative provides the boundary constraints on possible military moves against the new state and its citizens.

The third category of countermeasures are counter-settlement efforts. By this, I mean that the declaration of statehood, either in actuality or on the horizon, may propel the Israeli government into taking steps it would otherwise not undertake. On this the Labor and Likud parties differ sharply. A Labor government might simply turn over most of the West Bank to Hussein, while this would be unthinkable for Likud.

Possible counter-settlement moves include:

–turning over the West Bank to Hussein;

–maintaining troops at a few strategic locations in the West Bank, then proclaiming unilateral autonomy and withdrawing;

–allowing a Palestinian state to develop in Gaza, with some form of autonomy in the West Bank.

For our purposes, the question is: To what extent would these moves undermine a Palestinian state if it had already been declared, or block it if they preceded a declaration?

Turning over the West Bank to Hussein would be tricky. It would mean counting on Hussein to accomplish what the Israelis could not: a) ruthlessly to put down the independence movement and b) to win ultimately the acquiescence of the Palestinian population. Given that a Jordan which ruled over the West Bank and Gaza would be 75 percent Palestinian, it is likely that over time this would simply result in a much larger and more powerful Palestinian state. Thus giving the West Bank to Jordan is a risky move for the Israelis. But it is even more risky for Hussein. What is the king to do when the PLO converts itself into the provisional government and declares the existence of the state? Is he to stand against the entire Arab world and take on the burden of putting down a Palestinian independence movement? Why should he do this? It is no longer clear that Hussein would take back the West Bank. It is even less likely that he would be a party to crushing a Palestinian state that was already proclaimed.

As for the other two options, given Palestinian determination to go ahead with the proclamation of independence and with the building of the state, an Israeli-imposed autonomy/withdrawal is a perfect environment for them. Under these conditions it simply becomes easier for the Palestinians to construct their state. The Israelis could not find any Palestinians to run an autonomous government if at the same time there was a provisional government of the new state. Thus, these counter-moves make sense only if they are offered to the PLO or to the provisional government as an alternative. If such offers are made, they should be taken seriously, especially the second alternative of autonomy in the West Bank and a state in Gaza.

At some point one has to ask: What exactly is the difference between autonomy and a demilitarized state? There are important differences, but if autonomy is full and serious then the differences lie primarily in the realm of foreign affairs. A fully autonomous region would not be able to vote in the United Nations or enter freely into international agreements. But one could imagine an autonomy that would give the Palestinians control over the land, natural resources, economic development, civil and criminal legislation, schools and police, and would even provide for a symbolic affirmation of unique identity through flags, special passports, currency and stamps, with regulations forbidding the entry of Israeli military personnel except under special circumstances. Under these circumstances, the difference begins to look a bit like "You say toe-may-toe and I say toe-mah-toe."

Indeed one could even imagine a situation in which the Israelis withdraw to certain strategic locations and announce autonomy and at the same time the Palestinians announce the existence of the state, and a modus vivendi is worked out without agreement on what the status is. The Palestinians might say that they are humoring the Israelis, and that, if the Israelis want to say that Palestine is an autonomous region that is neither part of Israel nor an independent state, then that is fine so long as the Israelis withdraw their soldiers. And the Israelis may say that they are humoring the Palestinians, and that if the Palestinians want to call this autonomous region a state, this is okay with them, so long as the Palestinians do not challenge Israel on the matter of treaties with other countries and remain at least partially demilitarized.

It is impossible to say what might happen under various rubrics because so many different kinds of content crowd in under the same word. The only clear point of difference would arise if the Palestinians were to insist on a state with a powerful army and with the ability to enter, without restriction, into treaty relations with other states. But in that case we are talking about a very different situation. Moreover, all of this gets fudged in the difference between de facto and de jure arrangements. Many states live with de facto limitations on their sovereignty. Once again, one only has to think of the Finns.

Special Concerns

Question: What happens to the Jewish settlers under this plan?

The question should be divided into two parts, before Israeli withdrawal and after Israeli withdrawal. Before Israeli withdrawal the most important consideration is that contact with the settlers not lead to violence. Some, but not most, of the settlers are ideologically fanatical about retaining the West Bank. A small minority have even supported terrorist actions against Palestinians; some of these are now in Israeli jails, others roam free. Once the State of Palestine is proclaimed, it can be expected that some of the settlers will seek to find ways of preventing the state from taking hold. They may seek to generate a cycle of violence that will result in unrestrained efforts by the Israeli army to crush the Palestinians. The challenge to the Palestinians is to prevent this from happening. Several clear and rigidly enforced policies will help:

–No attacks, lethal or non-lethal, on settlers.

–A minimum of contact. Try to ignore them.

–In response to settler violence, try to get out of immediate danger.

–Use violence only in self-defense and when no other alternative is available.

–Publicize any provocative actions on the part of settlers.

If the Israeli withdrawal is part of a negotiated solution to the conflict then the settler issue will be dealt with in those negotiations. Probably the best policy for the Palestinians is to permit Jewish settlers to live and settle in the West Bank and Gaza, provided that they respect the laws of the new state. In short, they will be resident aliens. The Palestinian state will, no doubt, have non-citizen residents from all over the world. Most states do. There is surely no reason to discriminate against law-abiding Israelis who for religious or historical reasons want to live in the West Bank.

A different issue emerges with respect to land under the control of settlers. Over the years, large areas of the West Bank and Gaza have been transferred from Palestinians to Jewish settlers. In dealing with the land issue the Palestinian state would be well advised to go slowly in exercising normal rights. And while this may indeed sting, given the Palestinian experience with respect to land at the hands of successive Israeli governments, it would be wise to provide ample compensation for areas reclaimed from settler communities. This no doubt would be a subject of negotiations and is an example of another area in which the United States can play a useful role as a source of funds for ensuring ample compensation, both for Israelis and Palestinians. In addition, such issues may be linked to the rights of Palestinians to receive compensation for properties they once owned within what is now Israel.

It is extremely unlikely that any Israeli government will merely withdraw, leaving the settlers to the uncertain disposition of the Palestinian state. Thus, it would be wise for the provisional government to develop a tolerant and generous policy in dealing with the settlers, and to announce this policy at the earliest possible date so as to allay settlers' fears and to promote withdrawal. Once the Israelis withdraw, such policies will have to be adhered to rigidly. They will be symbolic of the new state's credibility.

Question: What happens to Jerusalem?

I have deliberately refrained from addressing Jerusalem thus far not because it is an impossible issue, but because Jerusalem remains a problem for all proposals that involve Israeli withdrawal from the territory gained in the 1967 war. Thus, U.S. policy does not recognize an Israeli claim to sovereignty over Jerusalem, and this issue would have to be dealt with even if there is no Palestinian state.

I have nothing original to add to the question of Jerusalem; political scientists can and will continue to develop numerous intriguing ways of dealing with the problem, be it creating a system of boroughs, conferring international status, or some other alternative.

Both sides appear committed to having Jerusalem as the capital of their state. This need not be a matter of mutually incompatible claims. If by "capital" is meant the place where the seat of government resides, there is no reason why some section of East Jerusalem could not house the central state buildings of the Palestinian state. And there is no reason why the Palestinian state could not exercise special rights with respect to these properties or regions. After all, every country exercises special rights over its embassy properties in foreign states; the United Nations has special rights over U.N. headquarters in New York; and the Vatican is actually a state inside the city of Rome. In short, the issue of Jerusalem turns more on the desire of both sides to find a solution, than on any intrinsic impossibilities.

Question: Does the strategy call for the Palestinians to specify, in their proclamation of statehood, exactly what boundaries they are claiming for the State of Palestine?

No. The Israeli Declaration of Independence does not specify boundaries, and there is no need for the Palestinians do so either. This is a judgment call. Against a specification of boundary claims are two considerations. First, this might become one more issue that the Palestinians would have to hammer out in advance. It could be a source of delay and discord. Second, it might be argued that since the Palestinians, per the strategy, will be offering to negotiate final boundaries with the Israelis, they would be in a stronger position in those negotiations if they entered them without having stated any specific claims.

On the other hand, an assertion of clear, limited boundaries that do not raise any questions of claims beyond the West Bank and the Gaza Strip would reinforce the Palestinian claim to be willing to live with Israel on a permanent basis and thus would help promote withdrawal and recognition. I find these latter considerations more important, and I would suggest that the provisional government make clear, either in the declaration of statehood or in a founding document of some sort, that no claim will be made for any territory other than the West Bank and Gaza.

Question: What happens to the Palestinians in Lebanon? What about the right to return?

When one asks Palestinians what they are struggling for, one usually hear two things: an independent state of their own and the right to return of the people who lost their lands. This, at least, is the answer at the rhetorical level. And it is expressed in the words of the first resolution adopted at the eighteenth session of the Palestine National Council in April 1987:

> Upholding the inalienable national rights of the Palestinian Arab people to return, to self-determination and to the establishment of the independent state on the national Palestinian soil with Jerusalem as its capital. . . .[3]

There is, of course, one small problem. If all the Palestinians (and their descendants) who lost land to Israel were to return to Israel, the Palestinians would constitute a majority of the population and would obviously be a threat to the state or, at the very least, to its Jewish character. Thus, the notion of the right to return carries with it echoes of the destruction of Israel.

This is known to everyone. The Palestinian call for comprehensive negotiations in which all issues would be resolved is an implicit statement of their intent to compromise on the right to return. In private conversations, the top Palestinian leadership will admit this, as will any serious student of the matter. On the other hand, compromising on the right of return is one of the most emotional issues for Palestinians, especially for those living in refugee camps in Lebanon. Palestinian leaders will not compromise on these rights prior to a full settlement establishing a Palestinian state, and they are very reluctant to admit publicly that they will have to compromise on these rights.

Where there is a will, ways can be found around such problems. For instance, the familiar distinction can be invoked between *having a right* and *exercising a right*. The Israelis are not threatened by a recognition of a right to return so long as there is no major exercise of it. Ways could be found to resolve this matter, but this will not occur prior to final negotiations. Some of the tools for resolution include compensation for land that was taken, Israeli acceptance of a symbolic quota of refugees exercising a right to return (after the 1948 war there was talk of 100,000 returnees), and provision to the refugees of a variety of attractive options including the right to become citizens of the State of Palestine with compensation, and the opportunity to become American citizens or citizens of various cooperating Arab or European countries.

With respect to the implementation of the strategy and the promotion of Israeli withdrawal, for reasons similar to those earlier advanced, it would be useful if the provisional government would indicate that even the right to return would be subject to negotiations. On the other hand, it would not be surprising if they passed over the issue or saw it as something to be dealt with in a final negotiated settlement some time in the future.

Notes: Chapter 4

[1] See Simcha Flapan, *The Birth of Israel: Myths and Realities* (New York: Pantheon Books, 1987).

[2] See Simcha Flapan, *Ibid.*

[3] "PNC Resolutions," *Israel and Palestine Political Report*, No. 133, May 1987, p. 16.

Conclusion

As I write this conclusion, the State of Palestine has not yet been proclaimed. Its creation is not far off. A unilateral declaration of independence and a proclamation of the existence of the state are steps on the diplomatic level that emerge organically from the Palestinian Uprising.

As I have argued, the Uprising is not a mere protest or rebellion. It is the very process whereby the Palestinian state is coming into being. For to create a state is to establish a mutual recognition of governing authority between a people and a law-giving entity. The Uprising has already destroyed the prior terms of Israeli governance over the Palestinians in the West Bank and the Gaza Strip. And at the same time the Uprising has bestowed governing authority upon the underground command.

Our thinking about statehood is too heavily concerned with physical issues. We suffer from a fetishism of territoriality. While sovereign control over a piece of territory is a standard feature of states, it is not the essence of statehood. The essence of a state lies in a social relationship among its members. For this reason the durability of the Palestinian state is in far less danger from Israeli countermeasures than many suppose. The Israeli government may be successful in preventing the Palestinian state from exercising many of the normal functions of a state, and Israeli troops may continue to occupy the country of Palestine for a long time to come, but insofar as the Palestinian people remain firm in their conviction that they have permanently bonded together in that form of human association we call a state, the State of Palestine will exist.

The PLO, as the organization that will soon be transformed into the provisional government of the State of Palestine, has made enormously significant shifts in its strategic thinking in a very short period of time. Yet the PLO does not fully experience itself as the soon-to-be government of an existing state. This is manifest in the fact that in its deliberations over the elements of a peace initiative it still thinks like a movement rather than a like a state. Movements focus vast amounts of attention on matters of fairness. They struggle with questions such as "Why should we make this concession, when they do not make a similar gesture?" But states do not think in these terms. They think in terms of national interest and national security. The highest duty of a state is to protect its citizens; and typically its most powerful drive is the preservation of its own existence.

It is unreasonable to expect that the PLO will begin to think like the government of a state before the state is actually proclaimed. But once the PLO takes this step, it will immediately undergo a transformation in its thought processes, its motivation, and its inner logic. The very moment it proclaims the state, the leadership must answer these questions: "What is our foreign policy? What is our defense policy? How will we preserve our national security in the face of the mortal dangers arrayed against us?"

It is this basic challenge of national interest, this responsibility of statehood, which will drive the peace initiative forward. There is no other viable policy of survival for the Palestinian state. It cannot defend itself by force of arms, and no outside forces will make sacrifices on its behalf. The only policy open to it is an activist pursuit of peace.

Another way of characterizing this policy is to say that the Palestinian state must adopt a policy of seeking political transformation within Israel. In characterizing the Palestinian defense policy as one of causing political change within Israel, it becomes clear that there is no such thing as a purely Palestinian defense policy. Political transformation within Israel is also a process that will have to engage the energies of tens of thousands of Israelis. And it is also a process in which the larger worldwide Jewish community has a role to play.

In short, the strategy articulated here is a single strategy for Jews and Palestinians alike. And I believe it is the only strategy that in the end will allow us to bring peace to the Middle East.